J. MacBride Sterrett

Reason and Authority in Religion

J. Macbride Sterrett

Reason and Authority in Religion

ISBN/EAN: 9783743351882

Manufactured in Europe, USA, Canada, Australia, Japa

Cover: Foto ©Lupo / pixelio.de

Manufactured and distributed by brebook publishing software (www.brebook.com)

J. MacBride Sterrett

Reason and Authority in Religion

REASON AND AUTHORITY

IN

RELIGION

BY

J. MACBRIDE STERRETT, D.D.

PROFESSOR OF ETHICS AND APOLOGETICS IN SEABURY
DIVINITY SCHOOL

GRIFFITH FARREN OKEDEN & WELSH
NEWBERY HOUSE, CHARING CROSS ROAD
LONDON AND SYDNEY

TO

Mother

THE

FIRST REASONABLE AUTHORITY IN RELIGION.

PREFACE.

Current discussions of contemporary religious themes and thinkers.

J. MACBRIDE STERRETT.

FARIBAULT, MINN.,
October, 1890.

CONTENTS.

CHAPTER I.

THE GROUND OF CERTITUDE IN RELIGION.

PART I.

Reason and Authority in Religion.

	PAGE
Discredit of Old Authorities	15
The Function of Criticism	16
Theories of Society Supplanting Theories of the Individual	20
Danger of Weak Romanticizing	22
The Right of Private Judgment	25
Ground and the "Urgrund" of Religion	27
Religion Genuinely Human	30
What is Religion?	31
Revelation	32
Faith	34
Sub-personal Conceptions of the First Principle	36
The Ultimate Conception of the First Principle	38
Religion Has a History	41

CONTENTS.

	PAGE
"I Believe" implies a "They Believed" and a "We Believe"	43
What Do I Believe?	44
Why Do I Believe the Catholic Faith?	45

PART II.

The Psychological Forms of Religion.

Three Chief Forms: Feeling, Knowing and Willing	49
1. Religion as Feeling	50
2. Religion as Knowing	53
(a) That of Conception	53
The Catechetical and Dogmatic Period	56
(b) Reflection, Criticism and Doubt	60
Saintly Doubt	61
Sinful Doubt	65
Faith as the Ground of Much Skepticism	66
Religious Knowledge Conditioned by the Incarnation	68
(c) Comprehension the Highest Form of Knowing	69
The Function of Philosophy	71
The Necessity of Religious Certitude	75
Philosophy of History	78
Philosophy of Religion	79

CONTENTS. xi

	PAGE
Modern Thought as Christian Thought	81
Use of the Nicene Symbol	82
Non-Œcumenical Theology and Theories	84
The Law of Liberty also the Law of Duty	85
The "Must" of the Bible	86
Open Questions	90
Inadequacy of Mere Theoretical Knowledge	93

PART III.

Religion as Willing.

This Rome-element Records Its Creed in Its Deed	96
The Moral Argument for Christianity	97
Instituted Christianity—the Kingdom of God	99
Mechanical and Ethical Conceptions of the Church	99
The Church and the State	100
Greek, Roman and Germanic Elements in Modern Christianity	102
The Christian Consciousness and Authority	104
Self-Consciousness and Certitude	107

CHAPTER II.

AUTHORITY IN RELIGION.

	PAGE
Two Notable Books on Authority in Religion...................................	109
The Authors of the "Lux Mundi".........	111
How Influenced by German Criticism and Philosophy, by Prof. T. H. Green, and the Oxford Hegelianism.— Their Appeal to Reason......................................	114
The Divine Immanence.....................	117
The Historical Method.....................	119
"Open Questions" Granted...............	127
Dr. Martineau's Previous Works; Their Character and Style.....................	129
His Bald Individualism.....................	134
His Critical Method and Negative Results...	146
Criticism of His Book by Contrast with the "Lux Mundi"............................	150
Bouleversment of this Party's Method......	154
These New Leaders Change It from a "Party" into a "School of Thought"....	158
Their Adoption of Hegelian Conceptions of Rationality, Revelation and Authority....	164

	PAGE
Two Criticisms of Their Work	178
(1) Their Conception of the Church too Insular to be Quite Catholic	178
(2) The Danger of Our Uncritical Restoration of So-called Catholic Customs, or the Vagaries of Ritualism	182
Welcome Their Spirit and Method, if not all of Their Results	183

CHAPTER I.

THE GROUND OF CERTITUDE IN RELIGION.

PART I.

REASON AND AUTHORITY IN RELIGION.

Discredit of Old Authorities.

"FATHER, don't you know that we left that word 'must' behind when we came to this new country?" This was Patrick's reply to a priest, who said that he *must* take his children from the public school and *must* send them to the parish school. This fairly represents the uttered or concealed reply of the mass of thinking men in the modern world to any presentation of the old authorities, when prescribed without further ground than an uncriticised imperative.

We have left behind the *must* of an infallible Church, of an infallible Bible, and of an unerring reason. Each one of these in turn has been abstracted from an organic process and proposed as the authoritative basis of belief. The inadequacy of the proof for such infallibility has rendered this claim of each one of no effect. The abstract reason, which was first used to discredit the other two, has fallen into the pit which itself digged, and *de profundis* rise its agnostic moans. Hence the task laid upon us in these days is that of inquiring whether these old *musts* do not have a real authority, other and more ethical than the one rightfully denied; to see whether they do not have a natural and essential authority that rational men must accept in order to be rational.

The Function of Criticism.

A criticism which is merely negative is both irrational and unhuman. The function of criticism is to be the dynamic forcing on from one static phase of belief and institution to another, to destroy only by conserving in higher fulfilled form. Its aim can only be to restore as reason what it first seeks to destroy as the unreason of mere might; to restore as essential realized freedom what it momentarily rejects as external necessity. Such work involves a thorough reformation of the whole edifice of dogma and institution, a thorough reappreciation of the genuine worth of these works of the human spirit under divine guidance.

Such a task implies an ideal of knowledge vastly different from that of ordinary rationalism. That holds an abstract subjective conception of truth, imagined under the form of mathematical equality or identity. It has no place for development or organic process, and none for comprehension of concrete experience which it vainly tries to force into its mechanical forms. This method, on the contrary, simply undertakes to understand *what is*, or concrete experience, under the conception of organic development in historic process. It can attempt no demonstration of the organic process of religion by anything external to it. It seeks only to give an intelligent description of the process. The process itself gives the conception of its rationality. It declines to abstract any part of the process or to seize any one of its static moments and make that the measure or the proof of the whole, as ordinary apologetics attempt to do. The real history of religion, then, like the real history of any organism in nature, is its true rationality and vindication.

The reason appealed to, also, is that which manifests itself in the corporate process, and not in the individual member. A religious individual is an abstraction. The truth is the whole concrete historical institution of which he is a member. Only as he experiences or mirrors the various stages of this organic life can he understand or express the rationality of religion. His certitude rests upon authority, which he, as autonomic, must finally impose upon himself. Ojective rationality can only thus become subjective and afford real grounds of certitude. Such a method of acquiring rational certitude may not satisfy those whose ideal of knowledge is that of ordinary rationalism. But have we not vainly tried to satisfy such an ideal long enough? Has not the century and a half of "the age of reason" landed us in agnosticism, from which it cannot extricate us? Are we not ready to abandon the attempt of such rationalism and try the higher method? This method consists of an historical and a philosophical study of religion.

The historical inquiry should first enable us to see the value of Bible and Church as records and aids of the religious life of the past. The philosophic inquiry should then enable us to see their necessity and worth to the religious life of our times. Neither of these methods is so irrational as to dare to sectarianize our religious life from that of the past. Both see this life as a continuous process, and only seek to understand and interpret what has been, as an aid to what should be. Neither of them are individualistic. Both of them study the individual as an organic member of the social whole, recognizing that the wisdom and the work of the many, especially as an organized community, is always greater than that of any of its members; reformers never being more than organs of the nascent communal spirit.

Theories of Society Supplanting Theories of the Individual.

The whole swing of the pendulum of thought to-day is away from the individual and towards the social point of view. Theories of society are supplanting theories of the individual. The solidarity of man is the regnant thought in both the scientific and the historical study of man. It is even running into the extreme of a determinism that annihilates the individual. Both **theology and ecclesiasticism have passed** through this extreme, which we may call the Chinese phase of belief and life. The Protestant world is slow to yield to the *Zeitgeist* heralding a retreat from individualism to socialism, dreading a repetition of its tyranny. But the swing of the pendulum has also begun in these spheres. "Martyrs of disgust" may be the loudest and foremost fuglemen in the retreat. But this does not prevent the heralds of concrete reason from advancing backward to reclaim their neglected heritage. The institution and the creed of the whole are being seen to have a rational authority that must be recognized. Society is seen to be the obligatory theatre for the realization of freedom. Its authority is seen to be that of order and harmony of individual minds and wills. No Church no Christian, no œcumenical creed no right belief.

But Church and Creed are already old. We cannot manufacture totally new ones. Nor can we accept the old forms at their old worth, as fetters of thought and action. We have outgrown *that* form of their authority, as the child outgrows the paternal authority. So we think. But the analogy is not perfect. Besides, the authority of the father as that of a full-grown man, which develops the powers of the child, is never fully shaken off. Nor does the individual member of a community ever outgrow the larger wisdom of the whole. At best the authority can only be translated from the form of coercive into the form of moral authority. And this is what we should aim at in our re-appraisement of orthodoxy and the Church.

Danger of Weak Romanticizing.

The danger of a weak romanticizing, of a pathetically pessimistic distrust of reason causing an uncritical acceptance of all the old bonds, should not deter us from seeking a *rationale* of them that will compel an ethical submission to their rightful authority. But it should put us on our guard against humoring a weak phase of the human spirit, which comes when its wings droop from weariness, so that a plunge into the ocean beneath seems relief. It should also put us on our guard lest the oncoming of this social view be permitted to take an abstract form, and thus crush out the might and right of personality. We should be alert to carry with us all the hard-won fruits of Protestantism. The danger is that we may find ourselves slaves again.

The two phases of authority for which Apologetics ordinarily contend are the intellectual and the practical. The first is that of creed or orthodoxy, the other is that of institution or Church. Till recently the burden of Apologetics has been the maintenance of orthodoxy, which has largely meant Calvinism, founded upon an unhistorical interpretation of an infallible Bible. Such Apologetics have had their day. They have almost destroyed both orthodoxy and the Bible. The other phase of Apologetics now claims to be heard. It claims to include the task of the former phase. The Church, as the author of the creed and the Bible, proposes to vindicate them as parts of its process—as its own offspring—in vindicating itself as the practical embodiment and promoter of Christianity. We need scarcely disclaim any sympathy with this phase as represented by Romanist and High-Anglican. The common method of both is arbitrary, abstract, unhistorical, dogmatic and unconvincing. It is the "must" which Patrick left behind in the old country. But Patrick never leaves his patriotism behind. He has a double sort of patriotism for both his old and his new country. He is unreflectingly wiser and more concrete than the abstract rationalist who owns "no tribe, nor state, nor home," nor content, except what he makes for himself. Nor can we leave the Church behind. It has helped make us what we are. The rational form of this method, then, commands sympathy. It should include a historical and psychological study of the institution, in order to arrive at a philosophical vindication of its rational authority over individuals, as constitutive of their essential well being. This affords a relative vindication of the various phases, and an absolute vindication of the whole process and its results. The end justifies the means, is immanent in and constitutive of these. But this process and result are in and through the community. Christianity is the Church. Its ground of certitude and authority is in the whole. It is in the light of this general conception of an organic social process that we must seek for the ground of certitude in both subjective and objective religion.

The Right of Private Judgment.

Certitude is conviction resting on discernment as a constant element in all the activity of our mental and spiritual faculties. The certitude resting on authority or on testimony really rests on a discernment of their reasonableness. Thus certitude is personal. It is the yea and amen of private judgment. It comes from the manifestation of the truth by God through *media*. In the case of religious certitude, the inclusive medium is the Church. But no doctrine of the Church as an organism that denies the right and duty of private judgment can remain an ethical one. Protestantism has bought this at too great a price to be bartered away. It is only as against an abstract individualism that ignores the patent fact that one is what he is by virtue of the social tissue in which he lives, that there is need of reasserting the authority of this constitutive environment. But this must be an ethical organism, inclusive of, and living only in and through its individual members. It is just as true that the Church exists in and through its individual members as it is that they exist in and through the Church. It is a kingdom of persons where all are kings, because all are persons, and not an abstract external authority. It is an organism of organisms, a person of persons, a Holy Spirit that only lives and realizes itself on earth through personal members. This much is said here to guard against any suspicion of reverting to the abstract conception of the authority of the Church as a ground of certitude, which was "the infinite falsehood" of mediæval ecclesiasticism.

Ground and the "Urgrund" of Religion.

I have used the singular, *ground*, instead of the plural, *grounds*, because what we wish is a vital organic universal, instead of a number of abstract particulars. "To be confined within the range of mere grounds, is the position and principle characterizing the sophists." (Hegel's *Logic.* p 196.) This species of accidental, arbitrary, special-pleading reasoning; this giving a *pro* for every *con*; this age of reason (of grounds) in Apologetics, had full sweep in the eighteenth century and far enough into the nineteenth to be responsible for much of the prevalent scepticism.

To-day, the ordinary grounds or proofs of our religion are justly called in question, and we are asking for a fundamental universal *ground* (an *Urgrund*) of them all—prophecy, miracle, the incarnation, the Bible, the Church, and reason—for the authority of all these authorities

This *Urgrund* must be an organic first principle which unfolds into a philosophy of religion as the only final and satisfactory Apologetic for Christianity; a first principle which vindicates religion as a genuine and necessary factor in the life of man, and Christianity as the fruition of all religion. Resting either in the simple faith of childhood, or on abstract external evidences, or yielding blindly to external authority by arbitrary wilful repression of thought, as did the late Cardinal Newman; none of these methods are possible to-day. Mere dogma and mere external evidences and authority are no antidote to doubt, no grounds of certitude in our day.

It is needless to multiply words in describing the patent phase of current religious thought. It is, in brief, one of unrest and doubt, and yet also one of faith and reconstruction. It is attempting the necessary feat of swallowing and digesting its own offspring of doubts. It is on its way to an *Urgrund* which cannot be something outside of itself. This can be nothing but the generic principle which, as constitutive and organic, is implicit throughout its whole process. At best there can be but an approximate comprehension of this immanent life-principle. But it is the task which the thoughtful human spirit feels as a categorical imperative. There is an underlying faith or certitude even in those phases where negative results are most conspicuous. **There is an everlasting yea** beneath doubt which alone renders doubt possible.

Religion Genuinely Human.

Religion is acknowledged to be one of the great human universals, co-extensive with man's history, and as varied in form as his culture. It is truly and essentially human. It is a necessary part of humanity's life. No religion, no man; perfect religion, perfect man. Organizations may decay and theologies crumble, but the religious spirit lives on through and above these changes, making for itself ever more congenial and adequate manifestations and organs of its perennial life—rising on stepping stones of its petrified forms to higher ones. With art and philosophy it forms the triad of man's relations with the Absolute Spirit. In these three inter-related and mutually sustaining spheres is exhibited the perfection of his spiritual character and functions. The creative object, the ultimate and constitutive ground of them all, is God.

What is Religion?

What is religion? A descriptive definition of the totality of phenomena which constitutes religion would be too extensive. So too would be a mere enumeration of the definitions of it that have been proposed. But most of such definitions have a common heart, and proceed from a varied reflection of a common truth. Religion is at least a conscious reverential relation of man to God. It may be "morality tinged with emotion," but that emotion must come from impact of the soul with God. It is a spiritual activity of self-relation to the great "Power not ourselves," through feeling, thought and will. It is a striving to fall upward from the mere physical side of our life. But this implies—and implies as its essential presupposition—the falling down, the self-relation of this Power to man. We must therefore define religion as *the reciprocal relation or communion of God and man.*

These two sides of this organic process may be termed (1) Revelation, (2) Faith. That is, the self relation of God to man constitutes the conception of revelation; the self-relation of man to God constitutes that of faith. The two elements are correlative, though that of God's activity is both chronologically and logically primal, and evocative of the other. Thus religion rests upon a universal. It is not merely subjective. We cannot abstract faith from revelation. For it is only both together that give us the concrete content of religion.

Revelation.

(1). Revelation is the moment of divine self-showing in the organic process which constitutes religion. As the self-relation of God to man, it is a primal and perennial act, which, in religion, is recognized as a phase of one's own personal experience. As *immediate*, it forms the background of all human life—sentient, mental and moral. It forms the *supra*-nature of humanity, and is creative of it. Back of, beneath, immanent in (μετά) all that is human, there is that which constitutes and sustains it. This metaphysics of man, mental and moral, is the immanent, immediate relation of God to humanity. But the term is generally confined to what we may call *mediated* revelation. God's self-relation to us is continually mediated and brought to our consciousness through our physical, mental, moral and social relations. He is immanent in these relations, and thus reveals himself to our conscious experience. It is through our knowledge of nature, through our knowledge and love of our brethren—that is, through our knowledge of the physical and moral world-order—that we become conscious of God's relation to us. Signs and tokens and mighty works, Bible and Church, family and social life, have all been used as *media* of this revelation. Revelation, however mediated, constitutes the *objective* side of religion.

Faith.

(2). *Faith* is the *subjective* side. It is man's conscious apprehension of God thus related to him through revelation. It embraces all the constituent elements of the human side of religion—the apprehension of the Godward side of all that we do or say or think. Faith is faith. This tautological definition is compulsory, from the nature of the activity. It is a primal, basal activity of the human spirit. It is the simplest, and yet may be the most complex, activity of conscious man. It has no special organ and is no special faculty, but is the dynamic in all our faculties. It contains elements of feeling, thinking and willing, because it is the *actus purus* prevenient and co-operating with all these faculties. It is the spirit's apprehension of realities through these faculties. It is its practical self-consciousness of the Absolute. It is the self practically conscious of itself, in its relation with God. Thus it is only another name for the highest phase of self-consciousness. Such self-consciousness is never merely *subjective*. Its contents are the results of the mediation of all its physical, social and religious environment and training, and ultimately of God, through these *media*. Religious faith—and specifically Christian faith—is God's children's cry of Abba, Father. It is their apprehension of their divine sonship, the responsive thrill of emotion awakened by the consciousness of God's paternal relation to them. Abraham's faith was his consciousness of friendship with God. Our faith is our consciousness of divine sonship through his eternal Son, Jesus Christ. Such Christian faith is a very profound and simple, and yet a most complex stage of self-consciousness. It involves the mediation of a Christian education, which implies that of eighteen centuries of the Church's life. Thus, while our faith is subjective and personal, it is only so because we have been educated into the conscious possession of the Christian heritage of centuries Our personal subjective faith itself, as well as objective faith, is grounded upon and mediated for us through institutional Christianity.

Thus the objective ground of religion is God, and the subjective ground faith—or the simple apprehension, through more or less media, of this relation—thus converting the whole into the process of reciprocal relations between God and man, which constitute religion.

Sub personal Conceptions of the First Principle.

It will not do to substitute for God " the power not ourselves," Law, Force, Substance, or any *sub*-personal category. And the non-personal is always *sub*-personal. It may be acknowledged that some scientific conceptions of law, order, nature, cosmos, are higher in one sense than some anthropomorphic conceptions of God, but they are never *supra*-personal, and can never afford the conscious relation we call religion. Our analysis of the content of consciousness can only arbitrarily stop short of that of self consciousness, or self-determined totality.

If the charge is made that our conception of the first principle as personal is merely subjective—the imaginative reflection of our own mind upon phenomena—it may at least be met by the counter-charge of the same subjectivism in scientific conceptions. Matter, law, force, are equally subjective measurements of the objective by the subjective. But this *argumentum ad hominem* is only a side thrust of thought on its way through and above all such imperfect conceptions of the first principle. All such conceptions are implicitly religious. They imply as their ground the full conception of God. Hence the scientist is sane only as he becomes devout. But this criticism of the categories of ordinary science, making explicit its real ground, is the work of philosophy proper. It is the needed corrective of scientific agnosticism.

Such a criticism of the categories of thought reaches a system of categories with God as the implicit and the ultimate one. We shall refer to this later on, but only superficially. Religion grasps this without reflection. Philosophy has nothing further to do than to point out the necessity and rationality of the human spirit reaching and resting in communion with this personal First Principle or *Urgrund*. The Incarnation, as the perfect realization of this bond between God and man, and the extension of the Incarnation in history, are the essential *media* of both present religious and philosophical apprehension of this generic *Urgrund*. In neither case is it reached directly or intuitively.

The Ultimate Conception of the First Principle.

Religion, then, as a part of man's consciousness, has its ultimate ground in the eternal and loving reason of the First Principle of all things. Faith itself, or the subjective side, is necessarily reduced to the action of the Divine Spirit in man. The consciousness of this actual vital relation, or reciprocal bond between God and man, is a primal and perennial fact, and the ultimate ground of religious certitude. Consciousness in man is implicitly a knowing of self with God (*con-scius*), and hence of knowing God in knowing self. This is the real significance of the ontological proof of the existence of God.

This bond is as real a relation as the causal relation. Indeed, it is often identified with this relation. Our heredity is from God, even though it be through lower forms of life, and our goal is also God, even though it be through imperfect manhood. The ground of religion we find, then, to be nothing extrinsic. It does not need a special handle in the way of external reasons. It is not founded upon nor sustained by the various alleged proofs. These may vary and pass away, but the activity continues as a necessary function of normal humanity. Religion will be found at the grave as well as at the cradle of man, because God is the immanent and transcendent essence of man.*

God is the ultimate metaphysics of man, physical, mental and spiritual; the real substance; the continuously creative and sustaining power in His offspring. The *Benedicite* is the spontaneous expression of the whole groaning and rejoicing creation. If men should be so insensate as not to worship, "the stones would immediately cry out" an anthem of praise. The Psalmist's exclamation, "Thou hast beset me behind and before; . . Thou hast covered me in my mother's womb," voices the consciousness of this ultimate metaphysics of all things physical. This *Ur-*

---

* "As the personality of man has its foundation in the personality of God, so the realization of personality brings man always nearer to God." —*Mulford's* "*Republic of God,*" *p.* 28.

grund is creatively present before consciousness comes to raise the new-born man above the brutes. It begets religion as soon as consciousness of this power, in however low a form, appears, binding man back to (*re-ligare*) or causing him to review (*re-legere*) the fact of this primal relation. This consciousness varies in degree, strength, form and clearness of content. But it is the ground of the various grounds that we can offer as causal of this, which is itself the cause of them. Prophecy and miracle, the Bible, Church and reason also, are all its offspring, and authenticated by it, rather than the reverse.

Religion Has a History.

But it is impossible that this fundamental fact of consciousness could be perfect at once. Religion, individual and racial, has a history. It begins as an immediate, indefinite apprehension of the fact in the subjective consciousness, but it expands and wins definite content with the growth of human consciousness in all spheres of experience. Thus subjective religion expands with new revelation and apprehension of it into objective forms of creed, cult and institution, which in turn educe and strengthen it. The same spontaneous consciousness of "the Power not ourselves" that led the childhood of the race to personify earth and sky, also led Plato and Clement and Hegel, through the mediation of Greek and Christian culture, to proclaim the essential and perennial kinship of man with God, in all the concrete experience of his life and institutions.

There is more than an analogy, there is a real kinship between the psychological and objective development in the individual and the race. So we may trace a common outline for both. Indeed its development in the individual is only rendered possible through connection with a communal life. It is only by a false abstraction that the religion of the individual can be considered separately. Here as elsewhere the universal is prior to, and constitutive of, the individual. But this is not an abstract universal. It is the concrete organism of which he is a vital member.

" I believe " implies a " They believed " and a " We believe."

One can say I believe (*credo*) only by first having joined with others in saying " we believe " (πιστεύ'ομεν). The *I* always implies the *we*. It equals to-day the socialized and Christianized man of the nineteenth century. I believe, because they— eighteen centuries of Christian kinsmen— have believed; and because we, the Universal Church, believe. Still, the subjective factor is central, and our socialized faith is *personal* communion with God. The individual has absorbed, and has been realized, not annihilated by, the universal. Religion remains to the end a personal relation to a Person, however much it has been nourished and quickened by the community. " I believe " now means the subjective, personal self-affirmation, "the everlasting yea" of our Christianized consciousness.

What Do I Believe?

But what do *I* believe? What is the definite content of the religious relation of the individual with God?

I believe the consense of the Christian consciousness in regard to God, man and the world. I believe "The Catholic Faith." We are far beyond the faith of childhood, of primitive man. The historic process of revelation and faith has rendered primitive immediate faith impossible and irrational. Both the act and the content have been endlessly mediated for us. Our consciousness of God has been enriched by that of a host of heroes of the faith, and by the cult and dogma of centuries of Christendom. Questions have been asked and answerd for us before we were born. We have been born into the heritage of these answered questions in the shape of the œcumenical creeds, though enough open questions still remain to make us heroes of faith, and our generation an age of faith. But *I* believe. This heritage of the Christian faith is mine, only by the subjective personal activity of appropriation and realization. The Creeds are the records of a series of deep insights into the content of the Christian consciousness. The mastery of these is an ascent of the individual into the universal—something that cannot be ours by mere rote-learning, but only as we think over, verify, re-create or experience anew within ourselves. Subjective faith remains the most important element of our spiritual life. We cannot be merely passive recipients of the most opulent heritage. And yet the universal, the objective, rightly claims its place. We see this, also, when we ask, further:

Why Do I Believe the Catholic Faith?

Why do I believe the Catholic Faith? What renders it possible for me to make this my own personal faith? Why does *my* faith, my consciousness of relation with God, have this definite form and content? This form of faith, though personal, is not an immediate consciousness—a primitive unmediated revelation of God. It is not a matter of mere individual feeling or intuition. The *why* can only be answered by reading the whole history of his development, through the interaction of subjectivism and objectivism, of the self and its environment. A fair analysis of this process likewise leads back to God as its ultimate ground. The psychological and historical lead back to this metaphysical *Urgrund*. This stage of what we call Christian nurture is an indispensable phase in the development of both strength and definiteness of faith. It is here that the rationality of authoritative catechetical Church teaching and Christian influence of family and community are to be justified.

It is chiefly in this *what* and *why* of religion that we meet with grounds that *seem* to be extrinsic and accidental. The task, then, is to translate these grounds into rationality; to discover their place, that renders them necessary and rational elements of the organic process of the relation of God and man. This task includes the psychological study of the development of man in the social organism, and the historical study of the development of the social organism itself, on the way back to the ultimate or metaphysical ground.

The faith, though once delivered, could never, from the condition of the case, even in Christianity, be once for all delivered to the individual or the community. This has had, is having, and will have a psychological history in both. *Faith* as an activity is forever the same, but its content, and the interpretation of this content, vary and develop with new conditions and culture. The life-giving Spirit inspires to some new form of practical religion, to meet new issues. The type of Christianity changes. Then the intellectual seers note this life, and modify the old theology so as to include it.

The question then is, whether the environment leading to change of both vital and credal form of Christianity can be justified; whether, in theological language, we can see the hand of Providence; or, in the language of philosophy, whether we can discern the immanent logic or reason thus objectifying itself in rational forms? Or, if we restrict credal form to the œcumenical symbols, and the normal ecclesiastical form to that of the primitive Church, the question is whether we can discern the rationality in the culture of Greece and Rome as well as in that of Judea, which makes "them legitimate ingredients in a catholic, complete Christianity." Can we, in other words, reach a philosophy of religion that justifies the multiform development of the two inseparable elements of religion—revelation and faith; God's seeking and man's finding; God's adhesion to man and man's adhesion to God? Such a philosophy of religion must be based upon a philosophy of history which must be simply a rational comprehension of empirical history. We thus indicate a work far beyond the limits of this present essay. We can do no more than note briefly the psychological forms through which religion passes in racial and individual experience, catching glimpses of the immanent rationality in the whole process.

PART II.

THE PSYCHOLOGICAL FORMS OF RELIGION.

Three Chief Forms: Feeling, Knowing and Willing.

We designate these three forms as (1) that of *Feeling*, (2) that of *Knowing* in its three phases of (*a*) *conception*, (*b*) *reflection* and (*c*) *comprehension*, and (3) that of *Willing*.

These are inseparable parts of consciousness, that we can only artificially separate for purpose of study. The *universal* element of thinking is more or less present in the *particular* element of feeling, and willing fuses them both into the concrete *individuality* of person or epoch. But in different ages and persons, and in the same person at different times, one or the other of these phases is more emphasized than the others. Hence religion varies in its psychological form.

1. *Religion as Feeling.*

Religion exists primarily in the form of *feeling*. Its genesis belongs to the primitive depths in which the soul is just distinguishing itself from the great not-self about it. It is the first coming into consciousness of the pre-conscious fact that every one is born of God. And yet this feeling is generally mediated by some religious instruction. The power behind and before is first felt, rather than known. This gives the sense of dependence, which always remains an integral part of religion. It may run through the gamut of reverence, fear, dismay and terror, or devil-worship. Or this power may be felt as a congenial and beneficent one, and the feeling run through the gamut of reverence, confidence, love, peace and ecstasy, or mysticism. Fear and confidence are the two marked elements in this phase of religion. There is no lack of certitude in it. The unreasoned certitude of feeling hallows any object, from a log of wood to the sky, from a Jupiter to a Jehovah. The fetich-worshipper has as much certitude as the Mariolater. All religions alike afford this certitude to their worshippers.

Historical illustrations of religions and of individuals in this phase will occur to every one So also will the names of Jacobi and Schleiermacher, who, in their reaction from vulgar rationalism, tried to make religion entirely a matter of feeling or of the heart. The certitude of this stage, I have said, is no measure of the worth of the contents of feeling. *De af-*

fectibus non disputandum. Schleiermacher went so far, we know, as to say that every religion or religious feeling was good and true; thus proposing a philosophy "as much contrary to revealed religion as to rational knowledge," and making anything like a communion of worshippers impossible. Each one has *his own* feeling, and this may be so emphasized as to lead to both sectarianism and atheism.

But, strictly speaking, this elementary phase of religion is quite indefinite as to what it feels. Until other elements enter in, there is no personal object given to worship. It represents the first conscious mysterious impulse toward the infinite and eternal. It represents those elements of reverence and confidence which made our Saviour promise the kingdom of heaven to children. But it is a phase into which other elements do speedily enter. The activity of the human spirit in relation with the Infinite Spirit impels it on to definite conceptions of God and content of feeling. Milk for babes, stronger nourishment for the growing child.

2. *Religion as Knowing.*

The phase of knowing in religion.*

We distinguish here three phases of knowing: (a) *Conception,* (b) *Reflection,* and (c) *Comprehension.*

(*a.*) *That of Conception.*

Mere feeling is rather an hypothetical stage of activity. Objects that produce feeling are soon named, or learned, or imagined. The child is soon initiated into definite religious conceptions which nourish his religious activity. This introduction into objective forms of belief and worship is congenial with his developing intelligence. It helps him to name and to imagine the object of his religious feel-

---

* I may refer to " Studies in Hegel's Philosophy of Religion," Chap. IV., for a fuller and somewhat varied statement and criticism of this *second* phase.

ing. The activity in this sphere is that of imagination. It is what we may call *mental* art—picture-thinking taking the place of picture-making. It is thought raising us out of sense. Here the object and the content of the religious feeling appear in forms corresponding to the degree of culture possessed. The new wine is first put into old bottles and then new bottles are formed out of the fragments of the bursted old ones. This mental art of picture conceptions advances, bodying forth in less sensuous forms and in more abstract language the content of the religious feeling they help to quicken. The savage indulges in rude sensuous art, or combines it with rude mental art, personifying earth, air and sky. The Christian child is met in this phase of activity with Christian names and symbols, which help him to higher conceptions of what he feels blindly stirring in his soul. They do not create, but only help develop his religious life in more rational form. The more abstract form of conception, *i.e.*, dogma, is of little use here, unless it be accompanied with parable, legend and narrative. It is the time that religion is nourished on narrative-metaphor. The Bible contains a good proportion of such food for the young, and Christian history, especially in heroic and martyr days, furnishes more. But these should be supplemented by current religious literature, comparable with that furnished our young people by *St. Nicholas* and *The Youth's Companion,* instead of the autumnal *leaflets* and childish Sunday-school books.

By means of literature the Divine Educator co-works in developing and strengthening the bond between himself and the growing child. Such narrative-metaphors are winged, and bear the young soul aloft to the very heart of God. It is the very sustenance for which young souls are hungry, and mere catechetical instruction in abstract theology is the veriest chaff to chafe and wither their aspirations, unless it be judiciously concealed in fragrant flowers or ripe fruit. Give them the luscious grape, and not merely the seed.

Along with this goes the religious nurture, through public worship, Church festivals and ceremonies. The Christian year, followed out as dramatically as possible, is the best teacher of Christian truth. Besides, all this brings out the social side of religion, and helps to unite them with God through uniting with their fellows.

The Catechetical and Dogmatic Period.

The time for abstract conceptions will come soon enough. The analyzing and comparing and generalizing activity will begin its work in due time. Here metaphors harden into fact or are generalized into dogma. The winged metaphor will be clipped. The seed of the ripe fruit will be sought. The soul will crave definite and systematic truth. Subjective feeling and its imaginative vesture must find a basis in " Church Doctrine and Bible Truth." Much of the non-symbolic teaching given, it is true, represents the work of this same phase of the activity of thought in Church teachers. Systems of theology are often not much in advance of this period of abstract conception.

How best to conceive God, and how best represent the essential religious relation in systematic form, is the question at this stage, as the earlier picture-form becomes more abstract. This is the time for positive catechetical instruction, mingled with sufficient personal and rational persuasion to win assent. The proper ground of certitude here is a mingling of reason and authority. The authoritative teaching of the Church, properly presented, is God's method of further development of the bond between himself and his children. What great Christian teachers and what the Church in œcumenical councils have framed, come as the most vocal angels of the truth.

Such teaching is the creation of the

Holy Spirit co-working with the communal spirit. It represents the best expression of a large Christian consciousness through many centuries. It can and should be given with authority. Grounded upon the vital idea of religion, it has a rational authority to which every member, at this stage, will gladly and unconditionally submit. Such authoritative teaching is the craving of the soul, and so essential to its religious life. Here such authority nourishes and quickens the religious life of the member, and submerges his individual conceits by giving him the one Lord, one faith and one baptism of the Universal Church. It is the time to go to school; the time when the mind craves teachers and longs for the wisdom that is beyond it. It craves to know *what* it ought to believe. It believes spontaneously on authority. It is also the time for Bible teaching, for Christian education through sacred literature.

The Bible is the Church's record of the

historical revelation upon which it is founded. It *contains* the word of God in all its forms of literature. It is also the *vehicle* of revelation to the inquiring mind and longing heart. Protestants have made no mistake in reverting to it as life-giving and authoritative. It will continue to be both of these when the fullest and freest Biblical criticism shall have done its historical, psychological and literary work upon it. It will be found to yield a much more wholesome authority than under its uncriticised form of infallibility.

Many may stop contented with imagination on the standpoint of Church services, with their symbolism and ceremonial observances. Others, less æsthetic, stop on the more abstract form of dogma, or orthodox belief. Vulgar Romanism and Orthodoxy illustrate these two phases of *conception,* of sensuous and mental idolatry, both of which are normal phases in the religious process.

(b.) Reflection, Criticism and Doubt.

The period of reflection. Reflection, indeed, forms a part of the activity which receives and forms definite religious conceptions and right belief. But it does not stop here. The normal activity of this phase impels on to a criticism of traditional and current conceptions on its way to a comprehension of the necessity of religion and an estimate of their comparative worth and real validity. Perfect representation or conception of God is intrinsically impossible, either in the form of pictured or of abstract symbol. Thought, in seeking this, has abstracted the essence of all its symbols or precipitated them into definite and logical forms, and annexed reasons thereto. The reflective activity now impels to an examination of these forms, and of the reasons alleged for them. It is essentially critical and inevitably skeptical It realizes the limitations and contradictions of attained conceptions. It then seeks to vindicate them by rationalistic investigations and evidences, only to multiply doubts.

Saintly Doubt.

This is a necessary phase in the life of every ingenuously thoughtful Christian and Church. It is the work of the spirit criticising its own inadequate creation. It is the normal activity of the human spirit responsive to new revelations from the Divine Spirit. It is not an alien force, but the implicit infinite energizing through and above the inadequate forms of its hitherto realization in the finite spirit. Such criticism is the normal activity of the growing human spirit responsive to the Divine Spirit's new revelation, of which it may scarcely be conscious. The *advocatus diaboli* cannot prevent the canonization of such temporary doubt as sane and saintly. Dogma making and dogma sustaining, straining, breaking and re-formation are all the normal work of the same phase of thought, as understanding, on its way to the comprehension of the concrete rationality of catholic symbols. It must reflect upon the various *musts* which have hitherto been controlling. It is the inherently just and normal demand of the human spirit to know the source and ground of these *musts*; to find a rationale of the authority of Bible, Church and reason.

The authority of Bible and Church may be rudely questioned by the reason that finally questions itself. Its aim is to see what it is in them that makes the Bible, Church and reason worthy authorities. Much of this criticism is directed against accidental, temporary and local conceptions of Christianity, which are inherently false to its spirit and purpose. It is the attempt to reconceive Christ under the changed conditions of modern science and thought. This task of reformation is laid upon many Christians and many ages. What we call revivals and reformations are only more emphatic workings of this spirit in the Christian community. It is the dynamic of the Christian *Zeitgeist* itself impelling to more comprehensive and vital knowledge of Christ, and should lead, on the one hand, to the throwing aside the accumulated rubbish of other periods, and, on the other hand, to the recovering and holding fast all that is good in previous forms of Christianity. From the mother's knee to the grave, from Bethlehem to the New Jerusalem, the Christian man and Church have this reflective, critical task to perform, in order to advance in Christian knowledge and life. It is a process of negating truth by affirming fuller truth.

Half of current scepticism comes from the pressing upon this generation outgrown conceptions and imperfect developments of the gospel. To acknowledge frankly the necessary imperfection of progress is not to detract from the gospel, but is to take away the edge of half the criticism. To attempt a readjustment of the letter to the spirit of Christianity; to reconceive

Christianity, if you will, in terms of modern thought and imagery; to put the spirit in new forms; to abrogate the old letter in its fulfilment in the new—something like this is the problem set for the defender of the faith to-day. To acknowledge that Christianity has often been bound up with false views of science, history, philosophy and politics, and with poor mechanical views of God, the world and man, and that to-day we are trying to free the spirit from these limitations and from the letter of theological and ecclesiastical dogmatism with which it has been unduly hampered, is to win sympathetic hearing and help, when otherwise we would meet with no vital response.

When this critical activity is abstract, it busies itself with finding grounds or reasons *pro* and *con*. It takes Christianity out of its concrete process and treats it abstractly as chiefly logical definitions. It proves and disproves and generally ends, unless it becomes concrete, in that negative form which should only be a mid station.

This abstract criticism is known as that of common rationalism. The *Aufklaerung*, *Éclaircissement* and *Rationalism* were the three national forms of the "age of reason." The eighteenth century should have sufficed for this narrow sort of mental work, and the nineteenth century should have gone on with the affirmative process. But it continues in its senile form of agnosticism. It has ultimately doubted itself as the organ of truth. Not much has been lost by this last stage, for its most positive result was a form of natural religion, or Deism, which dried up the rich fountain of spiritual life, having a God who was little better than "a frost-bitten reality."

Sinful Doubt.

It is only when the spirit's activity droops and stops its work at this abstract negative stage, that doubt can be called sinful. It is then putting the absolute emphasis on subjective reason. It is then non-human, non-rational, a violation of the binding relation between God and man through historical and social media. Such absolute negativity of subjectivism is the very essence of the devil. No one is more to be pitied and no one is more to be dreaded than the man who has stuck fast in the mire of this standpoint. The truly human cries out,

"Great God, I'd rather be
A pagan, suckled in a creed outworn!"

It is the natural penalty of thought abstracted from action and institution. It is the penalty of holding to Christianity as chiefly logical doctrine. For belief is rarely the outcome of formal logical procedure. Concrete Christianity is also Catholicism, as well as orthodoxy and Protestantism. The East and the West and the New West are only elements of its organic life. Attempts to vindicate any of these, abstracted from the whole, necessarily lead to doubt and disbelief.

Faith, as the Ground of much Skepticism.
Much of the prevalent skepticism, how-

ever, is earnest, serious, wistful, and not Mephistophelian. It is within the Church in which its martyrs have been nurtured. It is normal. Puritanism, in its day, and Anglo-Catholicism both doubted, protested and deformed as well as reformed the contemporary forms of faith and life. They appealed from a present to a higher conception of Christianity. The New Theology is but another illustration of the same activity. Faith is at the bottom of such work. It is the outworking of a higher conception of Christianity in the common Christian consciousness. The real ground of criticism is here the real ground of certitude in this transition epoch. It is faith's apprehension of a deeper and larger revelation breaking forth from fettered Bible, Church and reason. It is the spirit negating in order to reform its inadequate conceptions—often, indeed, only an effort to understand, that it may hold with stronger conviction its catholic heritage. In this is seen the infinite cunning of the guiding Spirit in spiritually minded men and in the Christian community. It is letting doubt have its way while using it as an instrument to accomplish higher aims. The normal end of such doubt is a comprehension of the natural and persistent co-relation and co-working of the Divine and human spirit in historic process, which explains and vindicates at comparative worth all previous conceptions and institutions.

Religious Knowledge Conditioned by the Incarnation.

This can, from the nature of the case, now come only from a genuine comprehension of the fact of the Incarnation and its historic effect in life, thought and institution. The religion o the Incarnation is the concrete form of reason that meets and fulfils the outworn abstract reason of this stage. It is born into a comprehension of that which is. Having proved to its satisfaction in agnosticism that its own subjective ideals were not rational, it turns to the real to find the concrete objective rational. If it arrives (at a comprehensive view) at a philosophy of history at all, it must find in the religion of the Incarnation the ripest and ultimate form of rationality. With Aristotle philosophy was a thoughtful comprehension of the encyclopædia of Greek life and experience; with Hegel it was the same speculative comprehension of the concrete experience of Christendom. That is the objective matter of this phase of the activity of thought which we have called

(c.) *Comprehension, the highest form of knowing.*

We are chiefly concerned now with the mode of its activity, rather than with its contents. Its mode is that of insight, system, of correlation of all relativities into a self-related organic process. It is philosophy looking behind and before all previous phases and comprehending them as vital elements of a totality. It is concrete experience taking full account of itself, winging its flight from both earthly and airy abstractions. It is the incoming of the tidal wave, to flood the little pools left here and there, and to restore their continuity with the great ocean. It is an overcoming of previous standpoints in one that correlates and embraces them all in a system which is self-related. It rises to the conception of the necessity of self-consciousness, which is perfect freedom. The heart of this system is the primal, persistent and vital bond between God and man, or religion. The result of its activity, as I have said, is conditioned by its subject-matter to-day. That subject-matter is the religion of the Incarnation; and philosophy only reaches its ultimate insight by a comprehension of that *which is*.

With many Christian thinkers the activity of the spirit does not persist unto this goal, where the wounds of reason are healed by reason; where the ground of authority is self-contained and self necessitated through a profound synthesis of them all. Either dogma or doubt catches and holds them. They remain in either one or the other of these phases of common rationalism. And yet the spirit's demand and possibility is to make this *ein ueberwundener Standpunkt*. Often it is only implicitly overcome. It is overcome in that vital act of faith which we may call abbreviated knowledge. It is overcome practically, but not in the way of thought.

The Function of Philosophy.

Philosophy is only the making explicit for thought what is contained in the ordinary Christian consciousness; only seeing the necessity of the real freedom in God's service; the realization of the bond between God and man contained in the consciousness of pardon, peace and communion with God through the incarnate Word. It is the discovery of the logic of the *Logos* in Christian experience and history. It accepts Christianity as the manifestation, the positive form of the absolute religion, affirming in its doctrine of the incarnation the essential kinship of the human with the Divine Spirit. It is the only thing that will save those who have passed into the critical, doubting stage, from either a hopeless skepticism or an arbitrary submission to a non-intelligent power, which is the essence of superstition.

Unsophisticated piety has no need of this. But how little of current religion is unsophisticated. How thoroughly the rationalism of the understanding has laid hold upon the majority of Christians. They are asking and seeking earnestly for reasons for their religion. Current apologetics, or external reasons, may temporarily satisfy many. But their inadequacy is also keenly realized by many others. They demand a sufficient reason, an adequate First Principle, which validates all proofs and authorities. Reflection, or the mere reasoning of the understanding, is incapable of reaching this. The only question then is, whether thought shall and can persist to its fruition, or whether the spirit shall faint in hopeless agnosticism, offering itself an unworthy sacrifice to either doubt or dogma. But here we must not neglect the value of the *practical reason*, the demand for religion in our nature, and the adequacy of current forms to meet this demand. We shall find that the theoretical can never reach its convincing result without inclusion of the practical reason.

In this work thought passes in appreciative critical review all the categories which it has hitherto used in rationalizing experience, impelled onward to an absolute First Principle which will include and explain them all; that is, it seeks for a self-related and self-relating system, or a science of forms of thought, some of which Theology, as well as Science, uses in its work. It is restless till it rests in a sufficient First Principle, adequate to explain all experience. Being, substance, force, cause, co-relation, external finality, an extra-mundane Deity arbitrarily creating and destroying, are categories which, when used as first principles, give rise to positivism, pantheism, idealism, deism and agnosticism. But concrete religious experience to-day is such as to render all such interpretations inadequate. The abstract supernaturalism of much theology, as well as abstract mechanical naturalism, has failed to reach the adequate conception of God which makes creation, the incarnation and restoration possible. Thought is restless beyond these conceptions till it reaches the thought of an Absolute Self-consciousness who manifests himself creatively in the finite world and man, binding them back to himself. It declines any conception which makes nature, man and God to be discordant and irreconcilable ideas. It is especially concerned to find the conception which binds man and God in the congenial bond which religion implies. Beginning with the individual finite mind, it passes through all the encompassing social circles, finding in the highest no place for " the religion of humanity." Religion demands a bond with a super-humanity.

Beginning with the conception of an abstract supra-mundane Deity, it passes through all theories of creation till it reaches the conception of the concrete absolute Self-consciousness that *must* create, and realize himself in his offspring. Abstract mechanical necessity, of course, is here entirely out of the question. It is the free necessity of his own concrete triune Personality which leads to creation and its culmination in the Incarnation. Such a First Principle contains in its very nature organic bond with his offspring.

The Necessity of Religious Certitude.

And in the light of this alone is finite

spirit, its nature, history and destiny, intelligible. Here religion is seen to be necessary. Its elements of revelation and faith are in the reciprocal process of the Divine Spirit to the human, and of the human spirit to the divine.

Philosophy does not create this conception of the First Principle out of nothing. It is not an abstract *a priori* conception. It is the logical ultimate and the chronological presupposition of all the other categories under which experience is alone possible for man. These categories or conditions of thinking can only be found by reflection upon actual experience. Philosophy is simply the science of these categories, implicit in the experience even of the most unreflecting, some of them becoming more explicit in the special sciences. It is not a knowledge of all things, but a comprehension of the underlying conditions of all knowledge in a system with an adequate concrete generic First Principle. Here its special insight is directed to the theological conditions of religious experience, or, in particular, of the content of the Christian consciousness as to sin and redemption, or of alienated and of restored communion (religion) with God through Jesus Christ. In other words, it aims at comprehensive insight into the rationality of Christian experience, or at philosophical theology founded upon historical and dogmatic theology.

It does not destroy or transcend religion, which is the most vital realization of the bond between God and man. Religion is the highest, the complete practical, reconciliation, and is not destined to lose itself in philosophy. Philosophy does not set itself above religion, but only above partial and conflicting interpretations of its experience. It leads us to know for thought and in thought, as reasonable and true and holy, what religion is as life and experience. It validates this experience for thought. It gives the highest authority to religion, by demonstrating its absolute necessity. It reaches the ultimate ground of certitude, which was only implicit and unthought of in the stage of *feeling*.

Philosophy of History.

It reaches, too, certitude as to objective religion. It sees the necessity and worth of all creeds and institutions as the outcome of the religious bond—the work of the spirit of man inspired by the Spirit of God in a course of divine education of the race. This spirit of comprehension is never envious. It often romanticizes, growing tender and reverent in its appreciation of the forms of the earlier stages in which it has been nourished. If it has passed thoroughly through the skeptical stage, it can never be ungenerous in its estimate of either dogma or doubt. Its insight into the truth of the heart of all religion; its ripe conviction of the necessary organic communion of God and man; its comprehension of the process of the Divine Education, or its philosophy of history, enables it to find itself, to make itself at home at the humblest domestic altar as well as in the grandest cathedral, always holding the critical faculty in abeyance, as having been satisfied once for all. It thus gives the highest authority in religion, as deduced from and implied in itself, as necessary. Holy and reverent is this spirit of insight, for it is the very Spirit of God which has bound the devil of doubt—a

" **Part of that power, not understood,**
 Which always wills the bad, and always works the good."

Philosophy of Religion.

It does not place itself above religion, again, because it is the child of religion. It reaches its conception of God only because religion has already realized the essential bond between God and man. In particular, it is the child of Christianity— the thoughtful comprehension of its own experience. This starts from the culmination of the historical manifestation of the bond between God and man. Jesus Christ manifested this bond perfectly. He was a man manifesting perfect absolute union with God. Rational truth can only be apprehended on condition of its existence in natural and secular form. It must be immanent in a historical process. The man Jesus did not primarily appeal to thought. He lived his practical life in the world. He came unto his own, and won them by his life. He became the fulfilment of the supernatural order implicit in all previous history, the consummation of the self-necessitated Divine act of creation in time. Here the hitherto immanent and constitutional co-working of God with man came to perfect manifestation. God became man because humanity was an essential phase of his own life. Here his perfect self-consciousness was manifested. Son of man and Son of God were manifested as congenial and inherent parts of the Divine Self-consciousness. Here was reached the axis of the world's history, or, for what concerns us at present, the axis of the world's *thought* about God and man; for we are still abstracting the concrete thought from the more concrete process of Christian life and institution.

Modern Thought as Christian Thought.

Christian thought, which is modern thought, starts from the sensuous life of Christ and continues following the secular extension of this life in humanity. This has been the woof of which thought has been the warp in the concrete web of the modern world. Previous philosophy had been an attempted comprehension of the relation of God and man as manifested in human experience. With the advent of Christ came new and fuller experience. It did not appeal primarily to thought. The practical experience of this life and its extension in the life of the Christian community came first. But thinking is an inherent human necessity which continued in the Christian community. It was self-necessitated to reflect upon and express in intellectual forms the content of its experience. The thought activity was new only as modified by its subject matter. Thoughtful men, men trained in philosophy, became Christians, and Christians became thoughtful. Hence Christian doctrines, and ultimately Christian creeds. These represent the most catholic thought of the intellectual aristocracy of the community, thinking upon the content of catholic experience. They claimed the guidance of the Holy Spirit gradually leading them into all truth. The Nicene symbol represents the highest and the most œcumenical expression of this catholic thought. This gives its authority to the completed Nicene symbol.

Use of the Nicene Symbol.

There are parts of this symbol which can have their proper authority only to those who can think themselves into its definitions and see how it states ultimate thought. Such thought should be the goal of all Christian thinking or theology. But all such knowledge is an approximate development toward, rather than an actual attainment. In the highest speculative thought and in the most œcumenical creed we still know only in part. But, for the understanding of the Nicene symbol, this speculative thought is necessary, as is also a knowledge of the whole history of the age which gave birth to it. Hence its general use in public worship is not to be desired. Repeating, parrot-like, forms of sound doctrine without any conception of their sense, is a pagan custom that we need not encourage. The Nicene symbol has its proper use in church-councils and clerical meetings. But perhaps this would be too great a restriction. One can join with the great congregation of saints of the centuries in hymning this belief in the full divinity and the real manhood of Jesus Christ.

Non-Œcumenical Theology and Theories.

Our discussion implies a distinction between what is authoritative for comprehensive thought, and the much larger part of dogma which consists of metaphorical conceptions, partial theories and inadequate definitions which are local and transient—at best, only truth in the making. It is this portion, too, about which much of the anxious thought and controversy and doubt of our day is concerned. To this part belong theories of the inspiration of the Bible, of the atonement, of future punishment, of the method of the creation of nature and of man. *Must* I believe them? Do we believe them? Have they believed them? If so, which one of them, and why? Here the history of Christian doctrine can aid us greatly. It shows that none of these theories have passed through the œcumenical work of comprehensive thought.

To the doubting and harassed Christian

asking what *must* I believe as to many traditional and current conceptions, we may answer : Believe them only so far as, from a study of their history, you can see them to be necessary implications of the doctrine of the Incarnation. Take them at a relative rationality, as more or less harmonious with the general Christian sentiment.

The Law of Liberty also the Law of Duty.

The œcumenical creed is here a law of liberty. But it is also a law of *duty*. We not only may, but we *must* freely investigate the grounds and worth of all other conceptions. Biblical criticism and the theory of creation by evolution, the doctrines of the future life and of the atonement, the question of church polity and ritual, all are *open* questions, in the solution of which we *must* take our part. The authoritative *must* is here that of free investigation, instead of slavish submission.

The " Must " of the Bible.

Protestantism repudiated the unethical authority of an unholy Church, but soon yielded the same sort of blind reverence to the Bible. The change was not wholly a mistake. It was the most spiritual and ethical attitude that could then be taken. The evil grew out of the abuse to which all good things are subject. Superstition changed this living word into a dead letter. It was given the place assigned by pagans to their oracles, or by Mohammedans to the Koran. Bibliolatry became as real as Mariolatry. Orthodoxy was based upon a literal interpretation of an infallible oracle. Hence more than half the honest doubt of our day. Hence, too, the form of unevidencing evidences, serving only to increase skepticism.

But there is a reformation rapidly taking place in regard to the worth and authority of the Bible almost as great as that accomplished by the Reformation as to the authority of the Church. Only this is an intellectual, while that was a moral revolt. It may take generations to bring men generally to a recognition of the rightful spiritual authority of the Bible, as it has taken centuries to turn the tide of appreciation in favor of recognizing the rightful and necessary authority of the Church.

Certainly it is not to be overlooked that a total revolution has taken place in our day in the conception of the method of revelation and inspiration. Our Bishops, in their late Pastoral Letter, acknowledge that the "advances made in Biblical research have added a holy splendor to the crown of devout scholarship," and mention both "shrinking superstition and irreverent self-will" as earth-born clouds that tend to obscure its holy light.

We can barely indicate the reformed conception of the Bible which is rapidly replacing the old one.

The Bible is literature. It is sacred

literature. It is the "survival of the fittest" of the sacred literature of the Jews and of the early Christians. Like the creeds, it is the product of the Church, and at the same time the fountain and the norm of Christian life and doctrine. It is a record of revelation done into history; a record of the historical incarnation of the Son of God, set in a partial preparation for it, and in a partial result of its primitive extension. It thus *contains* God's revelation. It is a vehicle of that revelation. It is itself a revelation of God to the student of it, and to the whole Church. It is not errorless, or infallible, or of equal value throughout. It is the Book of the Church to the Church and for the Church. Hence the Christian consciousness, rather than individuals, is the best interpreter of it. It also, in turn, produces and gives the norm of development to the life and doctrine of the Church. It is a living word, appealing to the mind and heart and conscience after criticism has done its utmost work upon it.

We still have the Bible. The Bible, and the Bible only, is the Book of the Church, and the rule of faith. But we do not have—or we shall not, when critical study shall have finished its work—a wordbook of equally valuable proof-texts, infallible *in toto et partibus*. This criticism demonstrates that the Bible is a record of divine revelation done into human history under the limitations of the mental and religious culture of the people of current times. All parts are not of equal value. Christ himself and his apostles criticised the morality and ritual of the Old Testament. Our Gospels are a fourfold transcription of inspired teaching in the Church of the first century. The Church was before the New Testament. It is the Church, founded and growing under the limitations of historical conditions, that gives us our authentic record of the life of Christ. But this is by no means to adopt the Roman Catholic method of setting the Church above the Bible. For it, in turn, is that to which the Church confesses itself bound to appeal to as the rule of faith. Good Churchmen now generally say that the orthodox view of the Bible as a verbally infallible text-book has never been a doctrine of the Catholic Church. I believe that Apologetics should frankly concede this, and thus free Christianity from the hundred criticisms that have force only as against such a theory—none whatever against the Bible as the Book of books.

Open Questions.

So as to liberty and duty in regard to other *open* questions. The greatest theologians of Christendom have always maintained this. Only zealots and party politicians have flourished an authoritative must over Christians in such questions. But this duty demands that we shall try to get at the heart, at the real significance of such conceptions and theories; to modestly seek to understand them before we dare call them irrational, after the short and easy method of many self-styled rationalists. Indeed, the historical method has largely replaced this negative rationalistic method even with unbelievers. They, too, thus find a relative justification for what they reject.* This much, at least, is compelled by the incoming appreciation of social and historical factors of individuals. One can only know through others, and ultimately the whole only through individuals. Thus historical and dogmatic theology furnish the necessary materials for philosophic theology. It remains true, however, that we can even thus only accept many traditional conceptions and dogmas in a Pickwickian sense. Our belief in them will accord with Bishop Pearson's curiously elliptical definition of belief as " the assent to that which is credible as credi-

---

*A very fine example of the historical study of dogma may be found in an article by Prof. C. C. Everett, D.D., on "The Natural History of Dogma." *The Forum,* Dec., 1889.

ble "—*i.e.*, belief is belief in that which is believable as believable.

But here we are still in the sphere of the liberty and duty of criticising inadequate metaphors and opinions. The task is how best to conceive or re-conceive Christianity through aid of past conceptions, and also through the aid of the changed conceptions furnished by modern science and culture. We cannot be chained to winged or to petrified metaphors of a past, whose whole material for imagination was very different from that of our times. We cannot accept them as authoritative, but must create the best we can, which will be as congenially authoritative to us as theirs were to them. More cannot be demanded. The modern ideal of knowledge is drawn on the canvas of a progressive education of the race. It is in accordance with this ideal that the most authoritative truth for one people or age may have but relative validity for another. Nor should the value of metaphor and abstract dogma as *media* of the divine revelation be overlooked in this criticism of their worth as scientific knowledge. Only we must not seek in them ultimate ground of authority. As we pass through self-compelled criticism from one conception to another, we are finding our real ground to be "the unity of identity and difference," of dogma and doubt. The new is better than the old only as it contains the old as a vital, though transmuted, element.

Inadequacy of Mere Theoretical Knowledge.

But even in the most concrete historical and philosophic view of truth we are still too abstract. We are studying Christianity as if it were chiefly a system of intellectual truth. We are abstracting the web from the woof, the *Logos* of the incarnation from the whole of its practical extension. We have acknowledged that Christianity must be done into history, into concrete life and institution, before it could be seen to be reason, just as the earthly life of Christ was essential to the seeing him as the *Logos*. Philosophy, then, must revert to this. Christianity is more than feeling or thinking. It is also deed. Theoretical cognition is not sufficient.

> "Grey, friend, is all theory; green
> Is the golden tree of life."

PART III.

RELIGION AS WILLING.

We have, then, to notice the third form in which religion manifests itself—that of willing.

Comprehension has to embrace not only the grey form of right thinking, but also the green tree of golden fruit—the extension of the incarnation in the practical life of the social body. Religion is not merely the feeling or seeing the bond between God and man; it is also the determination of life by the bond. It is willing to be God-like. This is the building power, the realizing of the extension of the incarnation to the sanctifying the whole of secular life. It is the Rome-element constantly accompanying or preceding the other phases of religion. It posits, puts in concrete form the certitude of both feeling and thought. It is founded upon the rock of secular reality. It was present at the giving of the Law upon Sinai, in the formation of the Jewish Theocracy and building its temple, as it was in Rome becoming the imperial mistress of the secular world. This bed-rock certitude has never left itself without a witness and an organ in the form of institutions which have been the *media* of all our culture. This has been the activity of what Kant called the "*Practical Reason,*" or creative reason moulding the concrete into accordance with its norm. It does the truth, and thus creates the forms which in turn nourish and educate it.

This Rome-element Records Its Creed in Its Deed.

This Rome-element, or the "Practical Reason," is eternal, always placing itself above past history by making new history, but always vindicating past history by the new which that past alone makes possible. It may be called the petrifying element of religion. It catches and fixes in progressive stationary form the fleeting phase of feeling and the restless dialectic of thought, and yet ever uses the new and more ample materials they furnish for its work.

Man does what he thinks. Man thinks what he does. Man is what he does. If we were compelled to choose between any one of these abstractions, we should say, Man is what he does. The *will* is the man. It is the concrete unity of all the elements of man. Any act of will is the expression of the whole man as he is at that time. It is his character, his law, his authority, his certitude. Doing, he is ever organizing his self, and ever rising on stepping-stones of past deeds to higher ones. Doing, he knows the doctrine of God.

The Moral Argument for Christianity.

But man is social, and pre-eminently so in religion. The kingdom of heaven on earth has from the first been a social community. Its deed is its real creed. Hence the worth of what is called the moral argument for Christianity — its visible power in regenerating and softening mankind beyond all disquisitions of philosophers and all exhortations of moralists. This is also the truth in the argument that Christianity is a life of God in the soul of man, rather than a creed; an immanent regenerative power, a mystical presence that moves the homesick soul to find its home in God in the ordinary routine of secular life. This too is the truth in the argument from personal experience of the members of this social body. Christianity *finds* them, meets their religious needs, nourishes their spiritual life, proves its adequacy to human need in all joyful and trying experiences. Its conceptions of life, of duty, of forgiveness, of eternal life—all the deeper moral and religious needs of the human heart—are met in the presentation of the Gospel by the Church to its members. This social religion is a religion of both inspiration and consolation. The Church meets and incorporates the new-born babe into its motherly bosom in holy baptism. Throughout life it lifts up its perpetual eucharist to meet his needs, whether he be crying *De Profundis* or shouting *In Excelsis*. At death it transfers him from the home below to the home above—from the Church militant to the Church triumphant. The certitude of these blessings comes from experiencing them. It is the deed of Christ's life in the members of his social body.

Instituted Christianity—the Kingdom of God.

But Christianity does not only realize itself in the practical life of its members, it also institutes itself in social organization. Here we approach perilous ground, or rather, we have to sail between the Scylla of an abstract universal and an abstract individual conception of the Church. What is the form of the Holy Catholic Church in which all Christians believe? We would fain escape from the strife of tongues by calling instituted Christianity the kingdom or the republic of God—the communion of saints on earth. That is the comprehensive truth. We limit ourselves to a few expository statements.

Mechanical and Ethical Conceptions of the Church.

Our conception of the Church depends upon our conception of the First Principle.

If God is conceived as abstract transcendence, the whole of religion necessarily receives a semi-mechanical form. Transcendence implies a dualism, a gulf, rather than a bond between God and man, that can only be bridged in a mechanical way. The incarnation and its extension alike suffer from this partial conception of God. Romanism is the standing illustration of the form of institution realized under this conception. High-Anglicanism is but its feebler counterfeit. This form has had, and still has, in some phases of civilization, its worth and relative justification. But to-day it is under the more genial congenial conception of the Divine immanence that we get the most comprehensive view of the kingdom of God as the whole of the faithful in every form of instituted Christianity.

The Church and the State.

There is no universal external corporate form that is inclusive. The Holy Catholic

Church is like the Universal State, that federation of nations and Parliament of man to which individual states are subordinate and organic, and which is the world's tribunal, to pronounce and execute judgment upon them. Though constitutional monarchy and Episcopacy be essential to the total corporate organization of Church and State, yet "one must needs be stone-blind not to see churches" and states standing without them to-day. The immanent Spirit was present in earlier forms, and now He is present in modern forms of Church and State, which have been inextricably interwoven throughout history. Protestant communions are also forms of instituted Christianity, closely in sympathy with modern states, which base their constitutions on the principles of freedom and respect for personality. Protestants necessarily regard the question of policy or constitution from a different point of view from that of Romanists. It is not an article of faith with them. The

Romanist conceives of instituted Christianity as a mechanical, unethical form of authority. We recognize its institution as an ethical and historical process of the spirit immanent in Christian nations and communities. This springs from our conception of the First Principle as concrete Self-Consciousness, or Love, self-necessitated to create, and to relate himself to his created offspring. It is a part of the philosophy of history which is quite modern, and yet Christian.

Greek, Roman and Germanic Elements in Modern Christianity.

Romanism is one phase of this process. But modern Christendom has passed beyond Rome as ultimate. It is largely Teutonic and Anglo-Saxon. Still it is only a part of a process which must conserve the Greek and Roman element. The Greek element stands for philosophy or orthodoxy, the Roman for law or polity, and the Anglo-Saxon for free spirit or ethical personality. Creed and polity are permanent elements which Protestantism must conserve with its free spirit, without being seduced back to the stagnant orthodoxy of the Greek Church or to the terrible tyranny of Roman ecclesiasticism. This is our task. It has its dangers, but it is a duty. The outworkings of the immanent spirit in our times indicate this trend of progress. The Christian consciousness is not content with so many Protestant variations. It yearns for unity.

We are still in the sphere of history in the making, but take our part in it under the conception of the Divine immanence. This conception is monistic and organic. It is the category of comprehension or of totality, self-active and self-realizing. Its chief danger is that of overlooking differences, instead of reducing them to organic elements. But it is the conception which steers clear of all subjective individualism, and is only consistent with the social view of man in all spheres.

The Christian Consciousness and Authority.

Thus it finds its ground of authority in the communal Christian consciousness, and strives to make this as œcumenical as possible. There are always relatively catholic orthodoxies, cults and institutions. These have been formative of every Christian person. Only in and through life in some form of them has he become a Christian. They have been God-given conditions to limit, in order to educe and realize, the individual. To be a member of some form of instituted Christianity is essential to one's being able to appreciate its rationality. It is from within such nurture that doubt may come to force him to wider conceptions or more catholic fellowship. Authority after authority, as teacher after teacher, may be transcended on the way to higher thought and life. But it must always be within some concrete form of the Christian consciousness that the authority and rationality of Christianity can be seen, on the way to comprehension and catholicity. The apprehension of its rationality comes after the experience of having our best-self educed by the process. The larger our fellowship, the larger authority and rationality we shall be able to recognize in this conditioning Christian consciousness.

Instituted Christianity needs and can have no grounds or evidence strictly external. It vindicates itself, as all organisms do. For comprehension, it is reason done into institution, the sum total of the outcome of the consciousness of the vital bond between God and man in historic process. Religion to-day stands for the recognition of the Fatherhood of God and the sonship of social man, till we all come unto a perfect manhood. The Church in every form is a partial organization of this recognition. Submission to its authority in the most catholic form is the rational submergence of our empty individualism in the whole historic life of the great brotherhood. This yielding is neither childlike faith nor unmanly superstition. It is the yielding that should come from comprehensive insight into the vital and constitutive relation of a concrete whole to the single member, subjective religion being rendered possible only within such a process. The historical is seen to be the constant accompaniment and educer of the psychological form of our faith, while both rest upon the metaphysical ground of the Divine adhesion to his own offspring in a course of education into full sonship.

To think ourselves into the creed, to form ourselves into the manners, to feel ourselves into the worship of the Church, is our highest rational duty. Such rational submission implies constant self-activity. This implies much doubt and much self-restraint. Hence it is vastly different from that servile, superstitious yielding to dogmatic external authority that rational

Christians will never cease to protest against as uncatholic.

Self-Consciousness and Certitude.

A person must always be at home with himself in the content of his self-consciousness in order to be rational. The creed and cult of the Church must be adopted and self-imposed through recognition of their constitutive influence in his own development. But this development he knows can never be in isolation. The rational for him is the social He lives and moves and has his being in and through social relations. The rational " I believe " thus rests psychologically and historically upon a " we believe." The rational " we believe " rests upon the Christian consciousness of the community of which we are organic members. This consciousness rests upon the primal and perennial vital bond of God with his offspring. Thus the ultimate ground of authority and of certitude is God's adhesion to man. The secondary, or mediating ground of certitude for the individual, is the Church, which represents the adhesion of man to God, through consciousness of this bond.

CHAPTER II.

AUTHORITY IN RELIGION.*

Two Notable Books on Authority in Religion.

THE two great books in the English religious world this year are Dr. Martineau's *Seat of Authority in Religion* and the new "Essays and Reviews," entitled "*Lux Mundi.*" They are both apologetical—the one for a minimized individual Christianity, the other for the concrete current of historical and institutional Christianity. They are both alike, too, in that their authors have read, marked, learned and inwardly digested the theological bugbear

---

* "*Lux Mundi.*" John W. Lovell & Co., New York. "The Seat of Authority in Religion," by James Martineau, D.D., LL.D. Longmans Green & Co., London and New York.

of German criticism. They are both also rationalistic, aiming as they do at establishing the rationality of *the faith* which they contend for, however great the variance between the contents of *the faith* in the two cases. But as regards the organ for interpreting Christianity, both acknowledge no diviner faculty than reason. They differ, too, but little in their emphasis of both faith and reason. They differ immensely, however, in the *quantum* of "The Faith" found to be rational, and in their conception of the rational.

The first volume is a painful surprise, on account of its minimum of content; the other is a pleasurable surprise, on account of its maximum of rationalism, in the best sense of the word. The broad becomes narrow and the narrow broad. Dr. Martineau, who, on his recent eighty-fifth birthday, received an ovation from the great and good of all creeds and classes in England, because of his noble "endeavors after the Christian life," here narrows the external concrete manifestation of Christianity to scarcely more than a half-hidden rivulet in noxious glades and arid deserts. The Anglo-Catholic movement, on the other hand, which has hitherto stood for appeal to uncriticised authority of a past, arbitrarily labelled holy; which has only spoken of reason with fear and hatred; which has narrowed the limits of the Church more than any Puritan; yes, the Oxford movement of Pusey and Newman here appears as not only offering but begging to appeal to reason, in order to justify itself to the times in which it lives.

The Authors of the "Lux Mundi."

Eleven devout scholars of the school of Pusey, "with unity of conviction," contribute the twelve essays in the volume, desiring "it to be the expression of a common mind and a common hope." They believe "that theology must take a new development," that "the faith needs disencumbering, reinterpreting, explaining."

Their twelve "Tracts for the Times" would have met with as severe condemnation at the hands of the authors of the Oxford movement, could they have been written then, as did the Broad Church "Essays and Reviews." The Rev. Charles Gore, editor, and one of the contributors, is the Principal of Keble College. His essay on "Inspiration" has already received a like welcome from some of the narrower and unprogressive leaders of the party. The common method and spirit of all the essayists are seen to be the attempt to reconcile the Church and modern thought, including modern German criticism of the *origines Christianæ;* to show that CHRIST is the true *Lux Mundi* of thought and science, no less than of religion.

Reason is the only interpreter. "Reason interprets religion to itself, and by interpreting verifies and confirms." Religion "dares to maintain that the fountain of wisdom and religion alike is GOD;

and if these two streams shall turn aside from him, both must assuredly run dry. For human nature craves to be both religious and rational. And the life which is not both is neither" (p. 90).

The Bible, the Church and individual reason are not three distinct messages or authorities. They must be so interpreted as to be seen to be but a manifold *one*—to be but parts of a concrete process. Separated from each other, abstracted from the process, each is alike false and misleading. Hence it is not each single man's reason or conscience that is ultimate ; nor is it the voice of the Church that alone proclaims the truth. It is the reason of the individual, informed, enlightened, rationalized by the corporate reason of mankind recorded in the Bible and the Church.

It is this which distinguishes their volume from Dr. Martineau's work. The authors have been trained and educated in the more concrete form of institutional Christianity. Dr. Martineau has, to a great extent, been separated from this life. He has been an eagle in the air, an Alpine climber on the top of the Jung Frau. They have passed their lives in the cool silence and holy music of cathedral choir, and in the book-lined walls of cloistered college, and yet also in the midst of the modern *Zeitgeist* that has invaded and conquered old Oxford.

How Influenced by German Criticism and Philosophy, by Prof. T. H. Green, and the Oxford Hegelianism.—Their Appeal to Reason.

The influence of German philosophy is even more marked than that of German criticism in their essays. A noticeable token of this is found in the opening essay on "Faith." In spirit and method it is scarcely to be distinguished from a lay sermon on "faith" by the late Thomas Hill Green (the Professor Grey of "Robert Elsmere"), leader of the Hegelian school at Oxford. The same is true of the essays on "The Christian Doctrine of God," "The Incarnation and Development," and "The Incarnation as the Basis of Dogma." In all these, it is true, the authors go much beyond Green, though not beyond Hegel, in starting from and remaining in the Divine reason done into the historical institution of the Church, with its Word, Ministry and Sacraments.

The influence of Oxford Hegelianism in these essays is very marked. The late Thomas Hill Green profoundly influenced many of the brightest men at Oxford, leading them to a study of Hegel. But very many thus influenced have been carried by Hegel's thought and their own environment into the Anglo-Catholic party. This has given rise to a current saying in England, that all the honey from Green's bees goes into the Anglo-Catholic hive.*

* Since writing this chapter I have looked over again the curious book of S. Baring-Gould on "The Origin and Development of Religious Belief," which was startling when first read some twenty years ago. I find it now, as then, a queer

But this honey has had the vital power to transform the hive. It is another case of the conquered giving laws to the conquerors.

hodge-podge of materialism and philosophy. The noteworthy thing about it, coming from an Anglo-Catholic, is its appeal to philosophy for vindication of the Christian religion, and especially its rapturous acceptance of Hegel's philosophy. Thus he says," The importance of Hegel's method I think it impossible to overestimate. . . . I believe that if the modern intellect is to be reconciled to the dogma of the Incarnation, it will be through Hegel's discovery." . . . "He supplies a key to unlock the gate which has remained closed to the minds of modern Europe. . . . I do not pretend to have done more than apply the Hegelian method to the rudiments of Christianity, to establish the rationale of its fundamental doctrine, the Incarnation." (Vol. II., pp. 39, 40, 116 and 375.)

However ill-digested the materials which he worked up, and however imperfect his apprehension of Hegel's method, he at least did pioneer work in calling attention to Hegel as a master in philosophy. I doubt not that his work has been one of the influences making "*Lux Mundi*" possible in that quarter. It need scarcely be said that their work is more scholarly and devout. Their style is rather German-like, while his is quite French-like.

The Divine Immanence.

The doctrine of Divine immanence is maintained as the Logos of the world both before and after the incarnation. Greek and Roman culture is received as "no alien element, but a legitimate ingredient in Catholic, complete Christianity" (p. 168). "The history of pre-Christian religions is like that of pre-Christian philosophy, a long preparation for the Gospel" (p. 171). The history of Christianity, too, is a long historical process of spiritual and mental assimilation and interpretation of the incarnation. Christianity, both as to its records and its creeds, has a history and is "subject to all the conditions of history and the laws of evidence." Historical criticism is welcomed as a true handmaid, a part of *Lux Mundi*. But historical conditions cannot invalidate the process they make possible. The word, the ministry and sacraments of the Church, though subject to all these conditions represents the real static elements in the process. They are the highest and truest expressions and interpretations of the *Lux Mundi*.

Neither history, nor religion actualized in history, is an unfolding of abstract thought. Feeling, fancy, desire and will are also elements of the concrete life, and the *Lux Mundi* recognizes, uses, is immanent in them. Parable and myth and legend, proverb, drama and poetry, no less than prose, are vehicles of his presence and power and beneficence. Christianity is not merely philosophy or theology or cult or creed or institution, but it is all of these, together with all thrills of feeling and visions of fancy and deeds of will that are inwoven elements of Christian history. Criticism may be welcomed to the task of distinguishing these various elements, but it must be dismissed the moment that it sets up any one or all of its dissected abstracted elements as the whole truth. The life and light, the *Logos* and the *Lux* of the world are in the whole. This spirit and method of studying and appreciating Christian history and institutions is notably that of Hegel. Indeed his impatience with the abstract critical study of religion is far greater than that of the authors of *Lux Mundi*.

The Historical Method.

Throughout Christian history, in which Church and creed and ritual and culture and life have been developed, "the entire human nature—imagination, reason, feeling, desire—becomes to faith a vehicle of intercourse, a mediating aid in its friendship with God" (p. 24). Welcome all that historical criticism may do to discriminate these elements, but hold fast to all. "Faith appeals to such a complex history to justify its career; it bears about that history with it as its explanation *why* or *how* it has arrived at its present condition" (p. 33). But mere "spiritualized Christianity" is abstract and evanescent. "The religion which attempts to be rid of the bodily side of things spiritual, sooner or later loses its hold of all reality. The Church of Christ is not so. It does not ignore the fundamental conditions of human experience. The incarnation was the sanctifying of both parts of human nature, not the abolition of either. The Church, the sacraments, human nature, Jesus Christ himself, all are twofold; all are earthly objective as well as transcendental spiritual" (p. 226). Hence the frank and unwavering maintenance of the creeds, ritual and ministry of institutional Christianity. They are bone and flesh and feeling and reason of these essayists; hence rational, in the highest and most concrete sense of the word. "There is one sense in which we may own that even the definitions of the creeds may themselves be called relative and temporary. For we must not claim for phrases of earthly coinage a more than earthly and relative completeness" (p. 212). And yet there is a sense in which they are final and authoritative, being "simply careful rehearsals of those inherent necessities which inevitably are involved in the rational construction of Christ's living character" (p. 41).

In the same way the Sacramental system is rightfully maintained as a vital part of Christianity. Its rationality and necessity are justly vindicated by far different methods from those which have hitherto been in vogue with the Anglo-Catholic party.

In short, no part of Catholic Christianity is given up, and yet no part is maintained by the former arbitrary method of mere assertion. The re-setting, the justifying the parts by their history and their helpfulness and rationality, puts an entirely new phase upon the whole.

There is nothing new in the modern thought and methods which characterize this volume. The only novelty is in finding them in the representatives of that party which has from the first most vigorously protested against modern thought in favor of what the early Fathers thought and said under Divine inspiration. The Bible "*contains*" the word of God, but is subject to all the conditions of history and laws of evidence (p. 35). "The modern development of historical criticism is reaching results as sure, where it is fairly used, as scientific inquiry" (p. 298). Even Christ, in his teaching, "used human nature, its relation to God, its conditions of experience, its growth in knowledge, its limitations of knowledge." Even the cry "remember Tuebingen" cannot frighten Mr. Gore from pleading for a free discussion of all these questions of Biblical criticism (301). All new truth of modern thought and science is welcomed as additional rays of the Light of the world, helping to interpret and to understand the Bible (p. 448).

Religion is to be interpreted and justified by reason manifested in a historical process of development. Morality is often far in advance of religion. The Reformation was a moral protest, a genuine moral revolt against a religion which had come to tolerate immorality. " True religion is rational; if it excludes reason it is self-condemned " (p. 68). " To say that a man need not interpret his religion to his reason, is like saying Be religious ; but you need not let your religion influence your conduct" (p. 74). Darwin and Huxley and Fiske present a wider teleology than Paley (77). Of a previous book of Dr. Martineau on religion it is said that " No more earnest and vigorous, and, so far as it goes, no truer defence of religion has been published in our day." Physical science and philosophy have destroyed the deistic conception so regnant in Christian thought. " The one absolutely impossible conception of God, in the present day, is that which represents him as an occasional Visitor " (82). " The conviction that the Divine immanence must be for our age, as for the Athanasian age, the meeting point of the religious and philosophic view of God, is showing itself in the most thoughtful minds on both sides" (p. 83).

It is admitted "to be the province of reason to judge of the morality of the Scriptures" (p. 89). They are not frightened by what some ignorantly stigmatize as pantheism. Three typical theologians of three different ages are quoted, "using as the language of sober theology words every whit as strong as any of the famous pantheistic passages in our modern literature" (60). It is frankly recognized that the orthodox thought has been cleared and served in no small part by "liberalizers." Such liberalizers are recognized as "helping to qualify the materialism or superstition of ignorant sacramentalists, or to banish dogmatic realisms about hell or explications of the atonement which malign God's Fatherhood" (p. 211). Such concessions to anti-dogmatists, as well as that of the merely relative finality of the creeds, are gladly granted "in the name of truth."

The Holy Spirit is the author of all life. "The Spirit claims for his own and *consecrates the whole of nature*. All that exists is in its essence very good" (273). The gradualness of the Spirit's method explains the most "unspiritual appearance of the Old Testament;" explains how, *e.g.*, Phineas' murder was reckoned to him for righteousness, and how Abraham obtained an even higher honor for being not a murderer only, but what was much worse, a child murderer" (pp. 274, 276). The same explains the imperfections, moral and intellectual, of the Christian Church, which has never been more than "a tendency, not a result; a life in process, not a ripened fruit" (276). As to the Trinity, it is said that "it was only with an expressed apology for the imperfection of human language that the Church spoke of the Divine Three as *persons* at all" (280).

The doctrine of the inspiration of the Scriptures is not conceded a place with *bases* of the Christian belief. Assent is asked in the Creed to certain historical facts "on grounds which, so far, are quite independent of the *inspiration* of the Evangelic records. All that we claim to show at this stage is that they are historical; not historical so as to be absolutely without error, but historical in the general sense, so as to be trustworthy" (284). Inspiration varies in degree, not in kind, in the teachers and writers of all religions and philosophies, and does not guarantee the exact historical truth of the records, as it is quite as consistent with myth allegory and poetry as with plain prose. Our Lord's use of Jonah's resurrection as a type of his own does not depend in any real degree upon whether that was a historical fact or allegory, Dr. Pusey to the contrary notwithstanding. Neither does his use of Psalm CX. guarantee its Davidic authorship (p. 300).

The visible method of the working of the Spirit of Christ in the world is made the historical and rational basis of the organization of the Catholic Church, with its Apostolic ministry. The rational ground for the succession of such a ministry is said to be "the necessity for preserving in a catholic society, which lacks the natural links of race or language or common habitation, a visible and obligatory bond of association." The *rationale* and extent of authority in the Church is the same as that given by Plato and Hegel. It is irrational when used for suppressing individuality instead of nourishing it, for the reaction of the individual on society is needed to keep the common tradition pure and unnarrowed (272). The number of granted "open questions," theological, ecclesiastical and liturgical, far exceeds that hitherto allowed by the previous representatives of this *party of finality*.

Open Questions Granted.

We have barely quoted some of the "open questions" and "concessions" granted by the writers of this volume. They will amply suffice, however, to show "the new front," the new spirit and the new method under which these new leaders present "The Faith" for the rational aceeptance of Christians of every name. The book, we would gladly believe, heralds a theological *renaissance* of genuine catholic import and extent.

The appeal is to reason, and awakens the affirmative response of reason. Such Catholics, *Anglo* or *Americano*, we would all gladly be. Such Catholicism we welcome as the need of the world and the Church to-day. It is the Catholicism of the nineteenth century after Christ—the *Lux Mundi* of our own day.

Such Catholicism is needed (1) not only to unify and inspire the diverse elements in our own Church, but it is also needed (2) to preserve, maintain and impart the heritage of Christian doctrine and worship that to-day has a diminishing hold upon the Christian world. It is needed to save from mere negative critical results, and from the baldest Quakerism, both of which are the conspicuous features of the other great volume—that by Dr. Martineau. A presentation of his results will afford us the best occasion for further reference to *Lux Mundi* as the genial antidote to the depressing, almost killing, negations of his book.

Dr. Martineau's Previous Works—Their Character and Style.

Dr. Martineau—*clarum et venerabile nomen*—has made a whole generation of devout and intellectual men his debtors. His volume on "*Endeavors after the Christian Life*" has been a genuine aid to faith and to personal piety. His volumes of "*Essays, Philosophical and Theological,*" have helped many out of the mire of empiricism and utilitarianism, and out of the murky limbo of agnosticism. His "*Hours of Thought on Sacred Things,*" though more analytical, subtile and subjective, still helped to wing the flight of the soul upwards "from the alone to The Alone." His more recent volumes on "*Ethics*" and "*Religion*" have been positive and constructive. Throughout he appears as an armed Christian knight, full of the vigor and joy of battle. He is a born warrior, but trained to fight single-handed, rather than as general in a large organized army. The Primacy of the English Church might easily have been his, if he had been a loyal member of it. He justly merited the marked ovation of respect recently paid him.

The marring elements of his intellectual work have been those which have helped to make it efficient—that is, his keen polemics and his brilliant rhetoric. A disturbing satiety of style is found in his last volume.

We wish that we had no other criticism to offer. It is painful to criticise one whom we have learned to esteem and love as a conservative helper in philosophy, ethics and religion. His radical critical attitude towards creed and church in this volume are unexpected and painful. But we are spared this pain throughout *Book I.*, in which he traces, with glad mind and heart, the evidences of God in nature, in humanity, in conscience and in history. Here he is positive and conservative, using his keenest weapons against materialism and utilitarianism. Here he commands assent and gratitude. Doubt is banished and faith is regnant. This part was written some eighteen years ago, for the extinct American magazine "*The Old and New.*" He had then collected materials for " a compendious survey of the ground of both Natural and Historical religion as accepted in Christendom." Released from preoccupation with philosophy two years ago, he found that his materials for the *historical* part—especially for the first two centuries of Christianity—had become untrustworthy. He set at work to overtake the advance made in historical research and criticism. The admirably lucid and full work of the German scholars made this a comparatively easy task. To this fresh study is due by far the larger part of the volume, which is so radically destructive of "The Faith."

It is scarcely just to pass over the first part of Dr. Martineau's volume without generous praise and extended quotation. It is a continuously profound, subtle and convincing argument for the existence and presence of God, as opposed to all materialistic and agnostic theories. The three grand discoveries of modern science, (1) the immense extension of the universe in space and (2) in time, and (3) the correlation and conservation of forces, may seem to banish God from nature. "But," asks Dr. Martineau, "is it not childish, then, to be terrified out of our religion by the mere *scale* of things, and because the little Mosaic firmament is broken in pieces, to ask whether its Divine Ruler is not also gone?" (p. 8). Again, "though natural forces have lost their birthday... they are no more entitled, by mere longevity, to serve an ejectment on the Divine element than the Divine element is to claim everything from them" (p. 19). The third conception of forces also leads to the theistic conception of the one supreme Will. All three of these modern scientific conceptions only serve " to elevate and glorify the religious interpretation of nature." And yet nature is "not God's characteristic sphere of *self-expression*. Rather it is his eternal act of *self-limitation*... the stooping of the Infinite Will to an everlasting self-sacrifice."

It is in humanity and humanity's history that his mind and heart are more clearly revealed. Conscience is the voice of God in the soul of man, divinely admonishing, inspiring, guiding humanity. In Christianity this voice of law is transformed into the voice of love. "The veil falls from the shadowed face of moral authority, and the directing love of the all-holy God shines forth" (p. 75). History shows us the stages of this drama of humanity and Divine Love. "Humanity is not only a *many*-LIVED organ; it is also a LONG-*lived* organ of God."

His Bald Individualism.

But we must turn from the part that will win praise and thanks from all good Christians to that larger part which will startle, pain, shame and anger nearly all who profess and call themselves Christians. For he puts forth as "approved" the whole mass of the most radical modern destructive criticism of Church, Bible and Theology. He himself thus estimates the results of his own work: "As I look back on the foregoing discussions, a conclusion is forced upon me on which I cannot dwell without pain and dismay, viz., that

"Christianity as defined or understood in the churches which formulate it, has been mainly evolved from what is transient and perishable in its sources; from what is unhistorical in its traditions, mythological in its preconceptions, and misapprehended in the oracles of its prophets. From Eden to the sounding of the last trumpet, the whole story of the divine order of the world is dislocated and deformed.

"To consecrate and diffuse, under the name of 'Christianity,' a theory of the world's economy thus made up of illusions from obsolete stages of civilization, immense resources, material and moral, are expended, with effects no less deplorable in the province of religion than would be, in that of science, hierarchies and missions for propagating the Ptolemaic astronomy and inculcating the rules of necromancy and exorcism." (p. 650.)

We need give but a brief résumé of the discussion leading to this almost atheistic conception of Christian history, before passing to a criticism of his whole conception and method.

In *Book II.* he treats of "*Authority Artificially Misplaced.*" His two antagonists are the Catholics and the Protestants, who "are possessed with the idea that they have actually got divine truth enclosed within a ring fence, still pure and integral after all these ages." They agree in having an *external* authority; they differ in attributing it, the one to a *corporation,* the other to a *literature.* As between Lambeth, Geneva and Rome, he decides that Rome has clearly the best right to the stupendous claim of being the Church, or the corporate keeper of the truth. Hence his first chapter is on " *The Catholics and the Church.*" No Protestant could wish for a more drastic criticism of its preferred " notes " of the true Church, i.e., *Unity, Sanctity, Universality* and *Apostolicity.* The Councils of Ephesus and Constance; Borgia, Tetzel and Torquemada — the whole host of blots on Christian history are so emblazoned over its pages as to render the text illegible. It presents the errors and superstitions and weaknesses of the Church, without the slightest appreciation of its organization, character and beneficence. With one fell, though long-continued and massive criticism, he destroys the Church of Rome, Lambeth and Geneva. He really polemicizes the Church under any and every form, and awakens sympathy rather than antipathy for the "mother dear" even in Roman form.

In the second chapter he deals like wholesale negative criticisms to "*the Protestants* and *the Scriptures.*" No Romanist would applaud his professed achievement of destroying the word of God contained in the Bible. To six of the epistles of St. Paul he allows merely *possible* genuineness. The synoptical Gospels wholly lack both genuineness and authenticity, being a mass of unhistorical accretions, false chronology, irreconcilable contradictions and fabulous conceptions. The Fourth Gospel was written in the middle of the second century by a Platonized Christian, who sought to prove that Jesus was the Son of God by transfiguring received traditions into philosophical realism.

We may spare the reader any detailed account of his criticism of the Gospels by quoting a passage in the latter part of the volume. This is from *Book V.*, which professes to be reconstructive. The first chapter is on "*The Veil Taken Away.*" This is evidently the heart of the book, the key-chapter of the whole volume. To read it is to know the whole work. *Ex uno disce omnes.* But we give the quotation first, though it occurs at the beginning of the next chapter:

"The portions of the synoptic texts which remain on hand, after severing what the foregoing rules exclude, can by no means be accepted *en masse* as all equally trustworthy. They are relieved simply of the impossible, and contain only what *might be true* " (p. 602). The italics are Dr. Martineau's.

In this *Book V.* Dr. Martineau reveals most clearly the Puritan, or rather the Quaker conception of Christianity that dominates his whole work. He constructs the historical Christ from his own subjective Christ. The Biblical, the ecclesiastical and the theological Christs are perversions of the " Light of the world " that has immediately shone into his mind. The nimbus and the corona are due to the refracting media through which the orb has shone. It is impossible for any true historical portrait to be produced. Christian theology and tradition and worship have only served to render the prophecy true to-day that his visage "was so marred more than any man's." Their cry, " Behold the God," renders it forever impossible for us to " behold the man." Yet even this perversion gives him a rule for separating the true from the false in the portrait of Jesus.

But what a Persian sword this rule seems to be ! What a *coup de grace*, beheading more keenly and surely than any guillotine! The rule is simply that of excluding "*all that men have thought* about his person, functions and office," and retaining "what Jesus *himself was*, in spiritual character and moral relation to God." Dr. Martineau goes on (p. 575) to assert that the Apostles and all Christian teachers in every Church, from the most hierarchical to the most reformed, have put forth their own thoughts about Jesus, instead of delivering to men *the religion of Jesus Christ*. [The italics throughout are Dr. Martineau's.] "We must not mistake all this scholastic dust for the divine radiance that shoots through it, and lends it a glory not its own." But, alas! he confesses "the real figure cannot, unfortunately, be seen by us except through the medium of human theories and prepossessions." Where then is he to find the real Jesus, when all these false accretions have been set aside?

He confesses that "it is perhaps a blind infatuation that impels us to seek, and a blind incompetence that forbids us to find such a portrait untinctured by some conceptions of our own." "It is in the subjective tincture of our spirits, not in the objective constructions of our intellect, that his consecration enters and holds us." Hence, " to draw forth the objective truth from behind this mist of prepossessions, we are thrown entirely upon internal evidence." Three rules may aid us in this hopeless task. I abbreviate, without marring, these rules.

1st. Reject all possible anachronisms, as where the narrators make past history out of present facts and fancies.

2d. Reject miracles that can be accounted for by natural causes, and the subjective conceptions of the narrator.

3d. Retain all acts and words ascribed to Jesus which plainly transcend the moral level of the narrators, and reject all such as are out of character with his spirit, but congruous with theirs.

"The first of these rules compels us to

treat as unauthentic, in its present form, every reputed or implied claim of Jesus to be the promised Messiah." "His investiture with that character was the retrospective work of his disciples" (p. 577). In his last days "his depression of spirit was due to his anticipation of rejection and martyrdom; not, however, as *Messiah*, but as *Messiah's herald* . . . he was simply the *continuator* of the Baptist's message" (p. 625).

So, too, the extension of the Gospel to the Gentiles was not embraced within the message of its founder (p. 585). Here, too, history is imagined back into prophecy by the apostles.

Dr. Martineau finds the application of his third rule "a much more difficult and delicate task for the critic." Here his own subjective preferences afford the only means of discriminating between the true and the false in the gospel portrait. Thus he finds "the self-proclamation of meekness and lowliness of heart, and the pompous elevation above Jonah and Solomon and the temple, are out of keeping with his personality." So, too, is "the irritation attributed to him by St. Luke against the obduracy of his own people," and also the unbecoming dinner-table invective against Pharisaic hypocrisy and ambition (596–599). There is finally left only "a few ineffaceable lineaments which could only belong to a figure unique in grace and majesty" (601).

The great part of the true story of Jesus has been hopelessly ruined in the transmission. Only "here and there a precious *shred* of it turns up at last under the eye of a far-off observer, who brings it unspoiled to light." Such shreds our author, the "far-off observer," tries to "bring unspoiled to the light" in his last chapter on "The Christian Religion Personally Realized." Here he says much that is fine and deep and spiritual as to the character of Jesus. The few lingering shreds of true history afford him *thoughts* almost too deep for utterance. Yet he has previously excluded "all that men have thought about Jesus" as unhistorical, and confessed the limitations of subjective conceptions. No wonder, then, that he adds, "As I look back on the foregoing discussions, a conclusion is forced upon me on which I cannot dwell without pain and dismay." How much more will his results bring pain and dismay to other Christians who thus find their Lord taken away, unless, like the first disciples, they find him not in the tomb, but appearing to them in the resurrection form and power of his holy Catholic Church?

Dr. Martineau, it should be said, does not believe in the resurrection of Jesus from the tomb. "The absolute conviction of this on the part of his followers is among the most certain of historical facts. But it belongs to *their* history and not to *his*, which has its continuance in quite another sphere" (p. 649).

What is left? "I am brought to a further conclusion, in which I must rest in peace and hope, viz., that Christianity, understood as the personal religion of Jesus Christ, stands clear of all the perishable elements, and realizes the true relation between man and God." But even Jesus' own personal religion does not imply that he was absolutely "without sin." As Mediator, Uplifter, Inspirer, "he needs only to *be better* than we are." And he is Mediator, "*not instead of immediate* revelation, but simply as making us more aware of it, and helping us to interpret it. For in the very constitution of the human soul there is provision for an immediate apprehension of God. . . And if Jesus of Nazareth, in virtue of the character of his spirit, holds the place of Prince of Saints, and perfects the conditions of the pure religious life, he thereby reveals the highest possibilities of the human soul, and their dependence on habitual communion between man and God" (Conclusion, pp. 651–2).

His Critical Methods and Negative Results.

We have endeavored to note faithfully the method and results of Dr. Martineau, and to abstain from running criticism. We have read *his* biography and gazed upon *his* portrait of our Lord with mingled pain and astonishment and resentment. We have spared the reader a résumé of *Book IV.*, in which he treats in the same negative way the various Christian "Theories of the Person of Jesus" and "Theories of the Work of Jesus." Suffice it to say that he does not treat the *thoughts* of Fathers, councils and theologians on these topics with any greater regard or conservation than he does those of the writers of the New Testament.

We have endeavored to be just, in order that we might criticise justly this work of a great devout man.

The title of this book is "*The Seat of Authority in Religion.*" But the field covered by his work includes (1) What is the ground of faith? (2) What is "*The Faith*," negatively considered? His substantial reply to the *first* is, that faith is faith, or an immediate apprehension of an unmediated revelation of God to the soul. To the *second* his substantial reply is that "The Faith" of Evangelists, Apostles, fathers, councils, creeds, theologians and Church is *not* "the faith," but only "illusions from obsolete stages of civilization," "evolved from what is transient, unhistorical and mythological," wholly concealing the truth.

It is this latter and larger part of his work that demands chief criticism.

(1.) A few remarks must, however, be offered upon his *first* topic—faith and its ground. Dr. Martineau is here a Quaker in religion and an intuitionalist in philosophy. He rejects all mediations as an obstruction and an impertinence. "Revealed religion is an immediate divine knowledge, strictly personal and individual, and must be born anew in every mind" (p. 307). He joins with those who ask us to set aside the divine influences transmitted to us by history, as impertinent obtrusions between the soul and God, and to retire wholly to the oracle within for private audience with God, though professedly acknowledging the danger in this position.

In his *preface* he also says, " I am prepared to hear, after dispensing with miracles and infallible persons, I have no right to speak of *authority* at all, the intuitional assurance which I substitute for it being nothing but confidence in my own reason." To this he demurs that *his intuitions* are *not his own* but God's—their source is Divine. This position in religion is certainly the *reductio ad absurdum*— one phase of Protestantism. It is to be noted, however, that Dr. Martineau is entirely unjust to Protestants, in not noting *his mark* of their reformation. He confines them to a *book-religion*, almost dishonestly ignoring their distinctive doctrine of *justification by faith* of the individual. The Protestant, however, is more just and rational than he himself ; for the Protestant does make this faith of the individual dependent upon, mediated by the Gospel records of the life of God in the soul of Jesus.

In philosophy this theory of immediate intuitional knowledge by individuals has had a history that ought to suffice to show its utter abstractness and untruthfulness. Mediation is the method of the universe and the life of the Spirit. The immediate—if such a thing is thinkable— is the crude, raw, uninformed, uneducated, uncivilized, unchristianized and unrationalized. We feel, we live, we know only through *mediation*, through relations to a surrounding set of mediations. Intuitionalism in philosophy, as Quakerism in religion, is a negation that only lives by surreptitiously appropriating all the mediations that it profoundly denies.

Let Dr. Martineau really blot out and unrelate himself from all the thoughts of evangelists about Christ and all the creed and deed of his professed Church, from the whole of the Christian sentiment, culture and civilization in which he has been bathed from earliest years, and he would be in some primitive stage of nature-religion, worshipping a log or a stone. Without the mediation of the Christian Church, history and life, he would never know there was a Christ, or have any loftier human ideal than a Hottentot. In philosophy he would be equally primitive, and therefore equally incapable and unworthy of a thought.

Criticism of His Book by Contrast with the Lux Mundi.

Yet Dr. Martineau's conception of faith as a personal conviction of relation with God is almost identical with that of Canon Holland, in the first essay in *Lux Mundi*. Canon Holland makes "faith an elemental act of the personal self," the motion in us of our sonship in the Father, the conscious recognition and realization of our *inherent* filial adhesion to God," " our personal intimacy with God." "To the end faith remains an act of personal and spiritual adhesion." Both Dr. Martineau and Canon Holland have the Evangelical or Protestant conception of faith.

II. Whence, then, the difference, when they pass from this to the concrete content which this faith receives and lives by? Whence the immense difference as to the amount and worth of " The Faith " as held by Dr. Martineau and the authors of "*Lux Mundi*"? The difference does not come, let us say, from either ignorance or rejection of German criticism by the authors of the latter volume. They have studied the same works with open mind. They have accepted the principles and many of the results of this criticism, and "plead that theology may leave the field open for the free discussion of these questions which Biblical criticism has recently been raising" (p. 301).

Every form of literature is conceded as entering into the complex of inspired Scriptures. "A considerable idealizing element in the Old Testament history" is recognized. Myth and parable, poetic and dramatic composition, are as much vehicles of Divine revelation as plain prose.

So also is the historical method welcomed as an aid to the explaining of the *how* and *why* of the form of Church polity, creed and ritual. The gradualness of the Spirit's method, the development through the imperfect to the less imperfect in all these forms is fully recognized. The Christian Church has always been "a hope, not a realization; a tendency, not a result; a life in process, not a ripened fruit." "The true self of the Church is the Holy Spirit, but a great deal in the Church at any date does not belong to her true self, and is obscuring the Spirit's mind" (pp. 276, 277).

The theory of evolution is also frankly

accepted, congenial as it is with the historical method. It is accepted as involving new ways of their attitude towards all knowledge. "Organisms, nations, languages, institutions, customs, creeds, have all come to be regarded in the light of their development, and we feel that to understand what a thing really is, we must examine how it came to be. . . . Our religious opinions, like all things else that have come down on the current of development, must justify their existence by an appeal to the past. . . In the face of the historical spirit of the age, the study of past theology can never again be regarded as merely a piece of religious antiquarianism" (pp. 151, 152). The physical, mental, moral and religious possessions of humanity, all come under the conception of evolution in harmony with the doctrine of the incarnation. Thought is alive, in movement in both God and man, "incapable of being chained to any one mode of expression; incapable of being stereotyped" (163). As to Christianity, pre-Christian religions and philosophy are recognized as positive preparations and contributions; "all great teachers, of whatever kind being vehicles of revelation" (165). So, too, every student in science contributes to Christian thought, "his discoveries being in fact revelations." All past religions, philosophy and science aid in "the progressive purification of the religious idea of God, till he is revealed as what he is to a thinking Christian people of to-day—the Object of reverent worship, the moral ideal, the truth of nature and man" (p. 56). As full justice is done pagan religions as could be asked by any impartial student. "In them Christ was schooling himself for incarnation."

Bouleversment of this Party's Method.

A more complete *bouleversment* of method has never been seen in any religious party. With these writers at least it has ceased to be a mere "party" and has become a "school of thought." They hold, with the Greek fathers, "the true successors of Plato and Aristotle" (p. 167), that "Christianity is a Divine philosophy and the Church its school" (p. 321). It has assimilated the Broad Church element. It illustrates, as Hegelianism itself has done, Hegel's dictum that "a party truly shows itself to have won the victory when it breaks up into two parties; for so it proves that it contains in itself the principle with which it first had to conflict, and thus that it has got beyond the one-sidedness which was incidental to its first expression." It remains to be seen whether or not the Broad Church school can assimilate the Christian heritage contended for by this party. It still *orientales*, not that it may stand gazing upon a fixed historical fact, but that it may trace the rays of the immundated *Lux Dei*. Thus, with Hegel these writers find in "this process of development and realization of spirit the true *Theodicæa.*" (Hegel's Philosophy of History, 477.)

Here, too, we find the secret of the immense difference between them and Dr. Martineau as to "The Faith." It is in their philosophy of history, which is that of Hegel. It is their philosophy of history which puts all the past in a new light, and compels them to stand by the accumulated heritage of the Christian Church. Here these writers rationally diverge widely and radically from Dr. Martineau. I have quoted Canon Holland's idea of the act of faith as identical with that of Dr. Martineau. But while he seeks to hold it in abstract subjective isolation, Canon Holland recognizes that it has had a history and a development. Faith necessarily acts and reacts upon all the complicated relations of life. It objectifies itself and gathers all its acts into a body, a creed, a cult. Faith begets "the Faith," as it apprehends the progressive revelations of its Divine Object. In an exercise of faith to-day we cannot "force ourselves back into primitive days and imagine ourselves children again." Our story has been a long and difficult one. Our faith has implicated itself with a vast body of feelings, fancies and facts. *The faith*, as we have it, is now old. " It has had a history like everything else, and it reaches us to-day in a form which that history behind it can alone make intelligible. Like all else that is human, it has grown. The details of events are the media of that growth. . . . But the history, which constitutes our difficulty, is its own answer. . . . We cry out for the simple primitive faith. But once again this is a mistake of dates. We cannot ask to be as if eighteen centuries had dropped out unnoticed—as if the mind had slumbered since the days of Christ, and had never asked a question. . . . Now we must attain our cohesion with God, subject to all the necessities laid upon us by the fact that we enter on the world's stage at a late hour, when the drama has already developed its plot and complicated its situations. This is why, in full view of the facts, we cannot believe in Christ without finding that our belief includes the Bible and the Creeds" (pp. 33, 37, 48).

These New Leaders Change it from a " Party " into a "School of Thought."

This is a very opposite way of appreciating history from that of Dr. Martineau, who rejects "all that men have thought about Christ"—all ideas that Apostles, fathers, councils, theologians and the Church have uttered about the person and work of Jesus, as perversions and hindrances to a true Christian faith. Dr. Martineau is abstract and unhistorical. They are historically concrete and rational. They hold the same as Hegel, who says, " It is important that the Christian religion be not limited to the literal words of Christ himself. It is clear that the Christian community produces *the Faith*. It is not merely the mechanical sum of

Christ's words, but the product of the Church enlightened by the Spirit."

With their philosophy of history, too, must be coupled their own historical edution. They have been born and nurtured in historical and institutional Christianity. They survey past and present Christianity from within the institution. Dr. Martineau's survey is practically from outside of such Christianity. He will not recognize it as bone of his bone and flesh of his flesh. It is this that prevents him from having a true historical appreciation of the Church, and causes him to regard its eighteen centuries of history as practically an apostasy from, an obscuration of, the *Lux Mundi*.

The characteristic difference between them is the same as that between Plato and Aristotle. Dr. Martineau, with all his splendor of imagery, subtile analysis and charm of language, is still "all in the air," like a man in a balloon, not going anywhere in particular. The others are working citizens and intellectual rulers in the *civitas Dei* beneath, of which he catches only glimpses and distorted views through the mists of earth.

Dr. Martineau is seeking for primitive, undeveloped Christianity. He wants to find the unfledged eagle in the unaddled egg. He is straining his eye to catch "the light that never was on sea or land." They are enjoying the light which enlightens and warms now, as it has eighteen centuries of Christian folk. They have suckled at the breast of the Christian social organism; he seeks to be a spiritual Simeon Stylites, rejecting all media between himself and God; a Christian Melchisedec, without genealogy. An old Grecian said that the best education he could choose for his son would be to make him a citizen in a good state with good laws. They have become good Christians in the same objective social way. They recognize their spiritual ancestry and home training. They have been loyal members of a good Church.

So, too, their conception of the Church and its history fits into a world-process and renders that process intelligible. His conception is so purely subjective that it has no place outside of himself, no consistency with any large historical process or institution. Even the Christ concealed by history cannot be seen, he confesses, without some distorting subjective conceptions of his own. Thus his own, as well as the corporate conceptions of the Church, hide what he would gladly find and use as an interpreter of his own immediate apprehension of God. His is the neo-Platonic effort at *ecstasy* which logically leads, as it has always historically led, to despair. Kingsley's spirited description of Hypatia's attempt is forever true on earth. They believe in the divine immanence, especially in the logic of Christian history, that the human spirit through eighteen centuries has no more been abandoned by God than has nature. This history has been but the actualizing gradually of the true nature of man through a practical assimilation and a rational apprehension of the image of God.

The history of spirit is its deed. It is objectively only what it does, and its deed has been the Christian Church and civilization. The true history of man is that of his institutions, and none is greater than the Church. He believes largely in the Divine absence from Christian history. His study of it is that which Hegel characterizes as *reflective* history, where "the workman approaches his task with *his own* spirit—a spirit distinct from that of the element he is to manipulate." Their method is that Hegel, "a thoughtful consideration of history with the simple conception that " Reason (Divine Wisdom) is the sovereign of the world ; that the history of the world, therefore, presents us with a rational process." (Philosophy of History, p. 9.) Indeed, one can read beneath nearly every line of their volume the inspiring conceptions of Hegel's "*Philosophy of History.*"

Dr. Martineau will certainly afford the chronic revilers of Protestantism, who know not Hegel, much less Christ, a good example of what they say is the logical outcome of Protestantism. We demur *in toto* to such a conception of Protestantism, which bears the visible *imprimatur* of the Divine blessing. But Dr. Martineau's extreme individualism and utter lack of historical appreciation certainly does call for a halt. Here is a decisive parting of ways. It is either concrete, historical, institutional Christianity, or it is nothing. The "*Lux Mundi*" essayists vindicate the rationality of instituted Christianity. They do not, like their predecessors and spiritual fathers, stop with an uncriticised acceptance of it, nor, like Dr. Martineau, with a critical non-acceptance. But they pass through criticism to a genuinely historical appreciation and a hearty acceptance of their Christian heritage. The Church has never yet realized its ideal, which however is its basis and goal. Like individual Christians, it has gone stumbling to and fro between its ideal and its caricature. "*Non adhuc requat hoc regnum.*"

Dean Stanley's "*Christian Institutions*" is the elder brother of their volume. It would be more correct, however, to call Baring-Gould's book the congenial precursor of "Lux Mundi." Dean Stanley's book so presents the historical environments as to make them seem to be the efficient cause and the just measure of the worth of Christian institutions. It lacks the philosophical element.

Their Adoption of Hegelian Conceptions of Rationality, Revelation and Authority.

Hegel's view of the authority of the Church, which Principal Gore quotes, is that of the dignity, worth and adequacy of the utterances and works of the religious consciousness of the ethical aristocracy of the community, as opposed to those of a subjective capricious individualism, which Protestantism is not. "The idea of the Church is this, that it widens life by deepening the sense of brotherhood; ... by checking the results of isolated thinkers by contact with other thinkers; and that it expands and deepens worship by eliminating all that is selfish and narrow, and giving expression to common aims and feelings" (p. 307). "It treats man as a social being who cannot realize himself in isolation" (269). He can become relatively complete only in social relations, and relatively a good Christian by being a good Churchman, as both Catholic and Protestant vigorously maintain.

If we are to choose, then, between Dr. Martineau's and their "Seat of Authority in Religion," we must, as rational (and as Christian) men, choose with those who may be accused of sanctifying all Christian history, rather than with him who may be accused of regarding it all as profane and atheistic.

The real is the rational. Institutions are greater than men. They are the utterances, or *outer*ances, of the Spirit, to educe the incarnate spirit in socialized man. *Unus Christianus, Nullus Christianus.* The Church is to the individual what language is to thought, what deed is to creed—vehicle and creator at once.

The conceptions of (1) Rationality (2) Revelation and (3) Authority which are regnant in this volume are thoroughly Hegelian. They steer clear of the abstract individualism, of which Dr. Martineau is a conspicuous type, and of the no less abstract socialism, under the form of arbitrary ecclesiastical authority.

1st. The reason appealed to is not that of the abstract individual, but that of corporate man, as objectified or done into history. The image of God, the true nature of man, is recognized as being gradually educed from humanity in historic process. Humanity is an organism on its religious no less than on its political side. And the eduction of rational religion is therefore through social religious institutions, rather than through prophet, reformer, or great religious leader or teacher. These are but the organs, the mouthpieces of the religious consciousness of the organism.

Hegel has forever made it impossible to appeal to reason, other than that of social man, expressed in his institutions. He has forever made it irrational to appeal to the subjective views of parts instead of the whole of the organism. He has brought back again the Greek ideal, only synthesizing therewith more justly the subjective element, making individuals organic members of the organism—making the organism an organism of organisms, the life of the whole throbbing through every part—instead of standing above the parts and mechanically ordering them into system.

To be himself, the individual must be social. To realize his own ideal he must realize the ideal of his community. On the other hand, the life of the whole can only manifest and realize itself through its organic members. The State and Church are the organisms which thus synthesize and live through the life of their members. They gather together and most completely represent, the one the moral, the other the religious consciousness of humanity. They are its objectified reason. To be a member of a good State and a good Church, then, is the only rational way of self-realization for the individual. They limit him only to educate and realize him, just as the family does the child. They are his true wisdom and his higher law.

This conception of corporate reason also leads to the *philosophy of history*, of which Hegel has been the chosen mouthpiece of the Spirit. It is simply that of the progressive eduction of the rationality of man in his institutions, in politics, art, religion and philosophy. It denies chance and affirms reason as regnant throughout history. It denies "decadence" and "cycles" of history repeating itself, and affirms progress in history. It denies continuous progress, and affirms progress by antithesis. It accepts with universalized significance the religious view of *Providence* in history. It declines to indite the whole, no less than certain parts, of history for unintelligibility or freedom from the control of immanent, regnant Providence. History is viewed as recital not merely of events, but of *intelligent* events—events in and over which Providence has been working.

This, too, differentiates it from the empirical historical method so much in vogue to-day. This perversion of the true method seeks to account for knowledge, morals, religions, and all institutions, by showing the historical genesis, or the empirical conditions in which they have been manifested. This is the method of Herbert Spencer, denying antecedent and concomitant rationality, or the teleological view. But teleology alone can account for rationality and progress. The true first cause, as Aristotle and Hegel have seen, is "*final cause.*" Both of them, and also the writers of "*Lux Mundi,*" quote with approval the first utterance of this truth outside of Scripture. That is the saying of Anaxagoras: "Reason (*Nors*) governs the world."

This conception of rationality in history leads to the recognition that the real at any time is the rational for that time—*e.g.*, the Mosaic economy for the Jews before Christ; and to the kindred conception that might makes right—*e.g.*, the Roman and the Christian domination of the barbarians. That is, Reason, or Divine Wisdom, has been able to "order the unruly wills and affections of sinful men." But it also forbids the ignoring of historical perspective. It implies degrees of better and worse, though "the soul of the world is good." It forbids any abstract re-affirmation, no less than any abstract denial of the ideals, faith and deeds of the past. "Moses said, . . . but I say unto you." It also forbids the mere glorification of any *status quo* of any existing form, as well as the uncritical acceptance of forms of the past. It does not permit a consecration of all the past history of the Church as ultimate, nor the idealizing of an arbitrarily chosen part of that history —the reverence "for a past that never was a present." It interprets the Church as the institution and organ of Christian consciousness. It is the progressive embodiment of the Divine idea as to man's relation to God on the side of emotion, imagination and devoted will. It is the standing record of the rational education of man on his religious side. It thus presents a series of increasingly adequate manifestations and vehicles of the *Lux Mundi,* positing successive forms, and successively transcending and fulfilling them in richer shape. It is the highest embodiment of the religious relation in corporate and institutional form. It is a complex of the Divine idea and of human needs, feelings, convictions and conceptions, through which the idea takes form and shines. It has a warp and a woof. The woof is not constitutive, as empiricists affirm, but the warp is.

> 'Tis that divine
> Idea taking shrine
> Of crystal flesh,
> Through which to shine.

The Church militant is the self-realization of Spirit in temporal process. All its merely temporal conditions do not account for its genesis and development. These would be merely chaos without the operative *Lux Mundi,* without the logical presupposition of creative Reason as the chronological antecedent and concomitant, or architect. In the beginning, and throughout, "was the Word." And yet the historical conditions which determined its form and progress were of divine choice and work. The world was prepared for the incarnation, and its subsequent development in life, thought and worship. The divine immanence lay back of chaos, protoplasm, and all the higher conditions—physical, social, intellectual and political—that have entered into historical Christianity. Without the culture of Greece and Rome as well as of Judea, Christianity could never have been what it is.

Both of these Hegelian conceptions of Reason as corporate and objective, and of the *philosophy of history*, have been so thoroughly assimilated by the writers of the *Lux Mundi* as to dominate all their apologetics for the Christian Church.

So, too, they are thoroughly permeated by Hegel's conception of revelation. On the Godward side it is manifestation; on the manward side it is discovery. All discovery made by man in any and every sphere of life and thought is revelation. All history is the record of man's seeking God, who had always and everywhere been seeking man. The rationality of history is but another form of statement for revelation. The modern rediscovery of the truth of God's immanence is really a revelation through philosophers and scientists. So, too, the poets of the Vedas and the Gathas, the Egyptian priest, and every man that cometh into the world, were vehicles of the Divine revelation, enabled, at least in a measure, to discover or spell out the manifestations of God (p. 170). Both the orthodox and the ecclesiastical conceptions of revelation have passed in music out of sight, in this larger conception.

The same is true as to their conception of *authority*. Reason is always and everywhere both the Law and the Lawgiver. Hooker's conception of law, its origin and sanction in its manifold forms, was far ahead of that of his times. These writers have not "shelved" him. His view fits into their conception of "The Religion of the Incarnation," and of the authority of the Church.

Their *philosophy of history* inevitably leads them to the maintenance of the authority of the Church over and through the individual. But it also modifies, *rationalizes,* their appeal to "hear the Church," believe its creeds, join in its worship, and practice its morality. This is especially noticeable in the essays on "The Christian Doctrine of God," "The Incarnation and the Development of Dogma," "The Holy Spirit and Inspiration," and "The Church." Extended quotation in proof of this is beyond our limits. The reader may refer to Mr. Moberly's interpretation of the Athanasian Creed (p. 215), to Mr. Gore's "perfectly simple idea" of authority (p. 271), to Mr. Illingsworth's answer to the objection that mutability and development of creed are opposed to its divine authoritativeness (p. 163), and to Mr. Lock on the authoritative teaching of the Church (p. 323-4).

Reason is "practical" as well as "pure." It is not a mere weak idea. It fulfils itself on earth by instituting itself in temporal forms. It has been thus fulfilling itself in and through the Church, which is therefore objective authoritative reason for every Christian. To be a good Churchman is essential to being a good Christian, a good man. In and through its social *ethos* man is to be confirmed and educated in the religious relation. It bears with it the marks of natural, rational authority of all God-given constitutive environments. Submission to its authority is the rational submergence of immediate subjective undeveloped individualism in the whole historic life of the great brotherhood of a common Lawgiver and Father.

So wide-reaching is this world power to-day, that in Europe and America it besets nearly every man behind and before. In the womb, school, cradle and society it conditions and stamps nearly every one with its genial mark. From the cradle to the grave it appeals to its children with the voice of paternal authority. It asks for no other than filial response and recognition of its past, present and promised beneficence in educing the religious relation implicit in man as man. This is the sort of authority ascribed to Church, creed and cult in this volume. Of infallibility and arbitrary or uncriticised authority there is scarcely a trace. On the contrary, it is maintained that *credo ut intelligam* is founded upon an ultimate underlying *intellexi ut crederem* (p. 189). The core of the authority of the Church is the fact of its being the adequate ethical and historical medium of the religious life.

Two Criticisms of Their Work.
Their Conception of the Church too Insular to be quite Catholic.

And yet one criticism must be offered as to their conception of the Church. It is too insular to be quite catholic. They do not use a map constructed on a sufficiently large scale, when defining the boundaries of the Church. The *idola tribus* still receives some homage in their modern Oxford. It is this which prevents them recognizing that outside of the Episcopal branches of the Church there are also other vital and fruitful branches. "*Hinter dem Berge sind auch Leute.*" Outside of the Greek, Roman and Anglican communions there are also Christian communions. The whole rich fruitful Christian life of modern Europe and America is a part of history. Their historio-philosophical method would seem to compel them to recognize and synthesize all this in their genial conception of the Church, in order to make it catholic, as well as in order to maintain their Hegelian philosophy of history—that history is not an apostasy, but that *Nors* governs the world.

Yet Mr. Lock feels compelled to draw a distinction within the limits of the baptized, between those within Episcopal folds and those of other folds, who are schismatics. Thus not only the Dissenters in England but Kirkmen in Scotland, State-Churchmen in Germany, Sweden and other countries, are ruled out of the Saviour's one flock, and the validity of their ministry and sacraments denied. They really base their apologetic for the Catholic Church upon its social religious power for good. Yet these other national Churches are as efficient forms of instituted Christianity and as valid powers for promoting the extension of the incarnation as the Church of England. They manifest the same historical vindication as the Church of Rome or the Church of England, as set forth by these writers. They are simply false to their spirit and method, in failing to integrate these forms as real organic members of the Catholic Church. In this they are neither historical, nor philosophical, nor Hegelian, nor Christian.* They have begun with the true catholic method of studying Church history, but they only partially realize the results to which this method will inevitably lead them.

This method looks at history as an eternal violation of law, because it is life and movement which destroy that which has been in fulfilling it—which shatters laws which have shackled the human spirit. Thus Jesus Christ violated the Law to fulfil it in the Gospel. Thus the Reformation violated the ecclesiastical law to realize a larger and more ethical extension of the Incarnation. This method of history must

* For a full discussion of this question of the Church, I may refer to my Appendix on Christian Unity, in "*Studies in Hegel's Philosophy of Religion.*"

be allowed proper scope or be denied entirely. This latter can only be done by those who set themselves above history—too busy building the tombs of the old prophets to see the new ones in their midst. The Church is always a means to the end of the perfecting of humanity. It meets new needs at new epochs with temporary or ultimate abrogation of laws hitherto essential to this end. Accomplished history indicates at least a temporary violation of Episcopacy as the normal type of Church polity.

If the development of Christian life in new forms since, and owing to, the Reformation; if this break with the old law seems like sinful schism, it is owing to a defective theory which needs replacing by a theory more adequate to the facts. A narrow, arrogant and formal Anglicanism is surely not adequate to the facts, nor to the work of restoring the old law of Episcopacy to meet the new life. And yet we look forward and work for this larger result. The integration of the new and the old, of Protestantism and Catholicism, is a goal that seems as necessary as it seems distant.

(2) *The danger of our uncritical restoration of so-called Catholic customs, or the vagaries of Ritualism.*

Another criticism, too, may be offered as to their conception of the so-called "Catholic heritage," which their party is laboring so zealously to restore. We find but little objectionable in the text of their volume, except this one narrow conception of the Church. We do not know how much of effete form and ritual they believe in adopting. But knowing them to be leaders of that party which has sought a restoration of all sorts of ecclesiastical rubbish, we feel tempted to read between the lines of the text and make them *participes criminis*. This revival of "catholic customs" by a party *ne plus ultra* Protestant dissenters is an incoming flood in our Church that needs to be met with some hesitating criticism. Much of it is unintellectual and unethical romanticism. All that can be done to really adorn the Bride of Christ, all the beauty of worship that is genuinely artistic and not tawdry ornament, is to be welcomed. But let this "be done decently and in order" by the Church, and not by the self-assumed infallibility of Protestant priests. Let it, too, be done apart from the desire to magnify the sacerdotal function of the presbyter above his ethical function as a leader and inspirer of men. The vagaries of individuals in this line in our Church far exceed the variations of Protestants, with their extempore methods.

Welcome Their Spirit and Method, if not all of Their Results.

However, we find no expressed desire on the part of these writers to be the promoters of mere ritualism. They seem to be thoroughly enough permeated by the historical spirit to avoid such nonsense. Let us take them at their text, as striving for the restoration of the organic and œcumenical elements of the Church, some of which we may confess have been neglected by Protestants. They are only seeking to restore as reason what had been given up because it appeared as unreason. This is but the return movement of history fulfilling by temporary or partial abrogation of old law. The Church is like the fabled Phœnix. Growing old, she fired her nest at the Reformation; but in the flames she is now seeking and finding renovation and development. We bid these new leaders of this movement all hail.

If the so-called Catholic party in our Church will follow these new leaders and interpreters of *"The Faith,"* they may become truly Catholic, and be in the forefront of the Church militant. If not, the party is doomed to the extinction which all isolation and lack of intelligence involves.

www.ingramcontent.com/pod-product-compliance
Lightning Source LLC
Chambersburg PA
CBHW032153160426
43197CB00008B/892